GOODS AND NOT-SO-GOODS
Consumer Economics for the '70's

GOODS AND NOT-SO-GOODS
Consumer Economics for the '70's

A. J. Rogers III

The Dryden Press Inc.
Hinsdale, Illinois

41,414

Preface

For years, books on "Basic Economics" or "Consumer Economics" have consisted largely of massive volumes of facts, figures, and numbers which have meticulously avoided any reference to concepts or theories. For some reason or other, academicians decided that anything theoretical was too complicated for beginning college students unless they were going to become economics majors. So textbook writers and teachers devoted their students' time to memorizing National Income Accounts and cookbook information on how-to-shop and when-to-buy.

This book has been based on the premise that basic economic theory is well within the learning capabilities of *any* beginning college student. It also assumes that an understanding of some elementary concepts will do more to make intelligent consumers than will the memorization of great quantities of facts and figures. Farily sophisticated concepts are presented, but no math or geometry is used except a few simple Venn diagrams. All of the theory is *verbalized* instead of *visualized*. For some students, this will be more difficult, but for others, the lack of graphs should be a big plus.

Questions are included at the end of each chapter, and generally these questions are quite different from those normally included in a consumer economics text. Some of them might find their way to a Ph.D. written examination, but this fact shouldn't scare anyone. As an old prof of mine used to say, "As you continue your study of economics, the questions don't change, just the answers." Hopefully, these questions will provoke some preliminary answers on the part of students. Again, hopefully the answers will provoke further questions and discussion.

As with most Dryden Press books, this one can be quickly and easily revised should the need arise. As author, I would welcome your comments, good or bad, about the book. The suggestions *will* be considered carefully for possible revisions. Students, this applies to you as well as your teachers. I can always be contacted by writing to Dryden Press, 901 North Elm, Hinsdale, Illinois 60521.

A. J. Rogers III
Beulah, Michigan

Contents

GOODS AND NOT-SO-GOODS
Consumer Economics for the '70's

PART ONE
Your Life Style and the Market

1. Basic Choice Sets

As far as we can tell, the world has been around a lot longer than the two-legged creature now called man. Theologians ponder, historians and earth scientists estimate, and poets sing about the beautiful blue and green planet that wasn't being all messed up by man and his struggle to "get ahead." Particularly in recent years, there has been an increasing tendency for all men to curse their very existence. "All our values have become warped," they say. "Not only do we pollute our environment, but we have chosen material goods as our exclusive gods."

The truth of the above statements is debatable, but one thing we do know for certain—man wants things. These things may be material, psychological, or spiritual; but man wants these *things* in addition to his own bare body. Dreamers have described utopian worlds in which man's wants were completely satisfied by the environment around him—a world which provided all his *wants* (notice, *wants* not *needs*) without his having to lift a finger. This would be a zero-cost world in which man could have everything he wanted without giving up anything else. Magnificent! But this isn't the case for men living in the world we know and have known. As man has become more knowledgeable about the world and his own productive capacities, he has been better able to meet his "needs" in terms of the basic food, shelter, and clothing required for minimum survival. The problem comes when somebody starts talking about "needs." The junior executive on the way up may *need* a ticky-tacky house in the suburbs to maintain his way of life. The redevelopment housing in the inner city may fill the equivalent *need* for the former tenement dweller. A shack in the mountains may provide a similar service—housing—for a hermit who has dropped out of society. The junior executive can tell you his needs. The inner-city resident can tell you his need. The hermit can tell you his need. No problem appears until the junior executive starts telling the hermit what the hermit needs or the hermit starts telling the core-dweller what the core-dweller needs. Now the moral question of who should decide *what* for *whom* raises its ugly head, and life gets complicated. Defining a need is almost impossible. Even if you talk about such a simple thing as minimum nutrition, no two people's requirements are going to be exactly the same. Wants are a different ball game. A person's wants are shown when he uses something when given the opportunity. If he is willing to give up one thing to get something else, the degree of his want is revealed. When everyone gets together and trades back and forth, these wants find a collective expression through the whole series of prices that evolve. Of course, these prices are usually expressed in terms of money given up per unit of the purchase, but this is merely a convenience. The money represents control over alternative goods, and the money price simply reveals how much of other things one is willing and able to give up for the thing in question.

Whether it should be the case or not, man's *wants* exceed his ability to fulfill them. This condition is called scarcity. There just isn't enough of everything to go around. Man's desires exceed his "satisfiers." Therefore, *choices* must be made between scarce items. Put another way, imagine all the desires of all men lumped together in a "universe." This is illustrated in Figure 1.1a as the larger enclosed area. In this world of desire, there are a number of satisfiers around, but they will only take care of a portion of a total desires. This is represented by the area-within-an-area in Figure 1.1a. Here you see the economic problem. Solving the economic problem can be handled in two ways and only two ways. Man can be forced or coerced to reduce his desires (Figure 1.1b). This method has been used with varying degrees of success throughout recorded history. Religious ascetics seeking the simple life effectively reduced the desire side of the equation—at least the desire for material goods. Mores set up by ruling elites have succeeded in reducing the demand for many scarce items. During the Middle Ages, it was considered improper for the serfs to eat white bread. The "proper" diet for the serf consisted of bread made principally from the chaff of the grain; the white bread went to the lords. This may seem unfair, but it sure helped solve the white-bread shortage, and with a minimum of cost. As another example, when my children were younger, my wife used to impress them with the joy of doing the dishes as opposed to the degrading occupation of watching TV. This con didn't last very long, but while it did the desire for watching TV was reduced and, at the same time, the satisfiers available (productive dishwashers) increased as in Figure 1.1c.

In a general sense, man's attempts to control his environment and increase his prosperity have taken the form of Figure 1.1c. We have constantly tried to increase the means of satisfying our desires. Figure 1.1c illustrates the situation in which satisfiers increase while desires remain constant. In actuality, however, this has not occurred. The satisfiers man can produce have increased at a prodigious rate, but man's desires have also increased in a seemingly endless game of the dog chasing its own tail. Whether this is "good" or "bad" is not the concern of this book. Our concern lies in the fact that man's wants exceed his ability to produce satisfiers of those

Figure 1.1
The Economic Problem

A. Desires exceed satisfiers

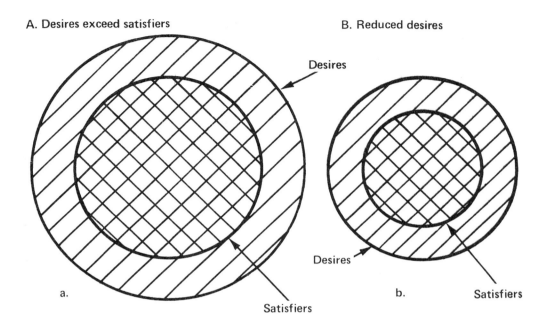

Desires

a.

Satisfiers

B. Reduced desires

Desires

b.

Satisfiers

Increased satisfier

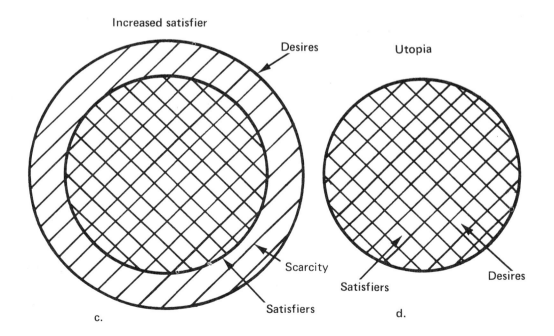

Desires

Scarcity

Satisfiers

c.

Utopia

Satisfiers

Desires

d.

wants. It is man's never-ending attempt to do so that *is* the study of economics. He strives to attain the utopia illustrated by Figure 1.1d, but he never gets there.

Throughout this book, much will be said about the role of information in the economic system. Having alternatives from which to make a choice is fine as long as there is sufficient information for choosing the alternative that will truly be most desirable. In a system in which economic choices are made for you, this information isn't really necessary. The choices lie with the decision-makers—not the individuals. A market economy, however, depends on the market participants having sufficient information to make "rational" choices. But what makes a choice "rational"?

Rationality, as used by the economist, merely means that individuals act in a way which will make their net satisfactions as great as possible. This doesn't necessarily mean that they will act in such a way as to maximize money income or even maximize pleasure. In some cases it may even mean that choices which will produce pain are made with full knowledge of the consequences. The martyr who died on a cross because he refused to deny his religious convictions may have acted with complete rationality. For him, the personal cost of such a denial would have exceeded the pain of physical death. If this martyr also happened to believe in life hereafter, the choice, while no less painful, would have been even easier. As another example, the masochist may derive satisfaction from hitting his head against a brick wall. While this behavior would *not* be rational for most people, for the guy who gets his kicks this way, such actions may be perfectly rational. In the sense that we will be using it, rationality is a completely personal thing. It refers to behavior by an individual as viewed by the same individual— not as viewed by the society in which he lives. Rational behavior, therefore, may be viewed as *irrational* by other members of a community and, as a matter of fact, one individual's rational behavior may impose substantial costs on other members of a community. (We'll see examples of this in the chapter on pollution.)

Anyway, rational decision-making depends *completely* on having sufficient information about the probable consequences of any alternative action. This may seem to be a simple-minded statement, but information is *not* a free good. Getting or providing information costs somebody something. Most of the everyday transactions that you carry out probably don't *overtly* involve large information costs. On the other hand, some do involve substantial information costs. The old joke about the housewife who spends a whole day trying to save a few pennies on some particular item is a case in point. If she literally has nothing better to do with her time, then the information costs may not really be too high. However, if she could have used that time to perform some other task of value to her or her family, then the information costs of a day-long shopping trip may exceed many times the value of her alternative occupation or the net savings she accomplishes.

Part of the purpose of this book is to provide *general* types of information about the consequences of many alternative actions you may be faced with in your daily lives. Compared to most books on consumer economics, this book contains relatively few facts and figures. It does, however, give you some thoughts that may help you find *and use* your own facts and figures.

One more item should be mentioned in this introduction. We live in a very uncertain world. I am almost positive that I will hit the next key on the typewriter right now. I am reasonably certain that I will finish the page I'm working on tonight. I am somewhat confident that I will finish the book by the deadline date. I am less certain (but *very* hopeful) that this book will sell like crazy over the next few years. My actions today depend to a *very* large degree on how I view the future. My *expectations* of the future play a big role in my *actions* today. Of course, this is true of everyone to a greater or lesser extent. The impact of risk or uncertainty on human behavior is very complex. Discussion of these aspects of economics usually is reserved only for advanced studies, but we're going to discuss it as though it belonged in kindergarten. Indeed, some of it does belong in kindergarten, but economists must make things complicated if they are to maintain their jobs, right?

Questions and Problems for Chapter 1

1. Using the diagrams developed in this chapter, draw the situation in which water (normally useful) becomes too abundant (a flood).

2. If you knew the exact date of your upcoming death, how would this knowledge change your choices today? Indicate any changes in "scarcity" as you know it using Venn diagrams.

3.   If everyone in the economy were to discover the exact date of their deaths, how do you think this would affect their present desires compared to the available satisfiers? Again, illustrate by using Venn diagrams. State the assumptions you are making. *Notice*, there may not be any "right" answers to the questions we're posing here. The answers will depend on the assumptions you make about human behavior. What you should be able to do, however, is to present *logical* answers based on the asumptions you make. Of course, the assumptions should be as close to real life as you can make them. What is being attempted here is to get you to *think* as opposed to simply memorizing a bunch of facts and figures. Through this process you can obtain *knowledge* as opposed to simple *facts*.

4.   List some alternative uses of *time* that you have had to choose between in the last month. Do the same thing for time alternatives between which you have had to choose within the past year. What is the most important choice (to you) that you have ever made? Why did you make the choice you did?

5. Now assume that you've just been given the word that you will live forever. Does this information affect your current view of scarcity? Illustrate with diagrams. What has now become less scarce? *Comparatively*, what has become more scarce?

6. Various revolutionary societies implore their citizens to sacrifice their individual wants to the greater benefit of the total community. What does this kind of request try to do? Illustrate with Venn diagrams.

7. List the costs, that is, all the things you and/or your parents have given up so that you can be attending school right now. List the benefits that you are receiving *right now* from attending school. List the benefits you expect to receive in the future from attending school now. *Given your own free choice*, would you still attend school now? Why or why not?

8. Is a mentally ill person rational? Discuss and define your terms. Compare and discuss your answers with others in the class.

9. "A bird in the hand is worth two in the bush." How does this person view uncertainty? Would you expect to see this person in a gambling casino?

10. If a person viewed time, both present and future, as being a "bad" instead of a good, what course of action might he take?

2. Economic Organization — Rights and Property

Why do we want to buy anything? While this appears to be a very simpleminded question, I wonder how many of you have really thought about it. Sure, we buy things because material goods and services can make our lives "pleasant" or "easier" or some other equally ill-defined adjective. Actually, however, we purchase things because of the *services* that we get from them. Think about it. You never buy something just to get the thing. You buy it because the purchase will allow you some kind of "right" to use some kind of service that the good is capable of yielding. If you buy a car, you are actually buying the right to use a particular kind of mechanical monster in particular ways. What are some of the services that cars might provide? Most obviously, you can usually obtain transportation from a purchased automobile. This transportation service may be valuable in helping you earn a living (if you're a traveling salesman, for example). Therefore, you would be willing to give up part of your other resources or buying power to obtain these transportation services. Maybe the transportation services will merely be used in running the family household—shopping for groceries, driving junior to the local school, etc. Still, these services are valuable in that, again, you are prepared to give up power to buy *alternative* goods in order to get the transportation services.

It may be that you wish to use the transportation services only to drive in the country for the purely aesthetic pleasure of seeing a beautiful sunset or a real cow in a pasture. The same principle holds, however. You are willing to give up something for the transportation services of the car. The services are productive even when the product is aesthetic pleasure.

Is transportation the only thing we get when an automobile is purchased? Of course not!

Were this the case, Volkswagen would have put Cadillac out of business long ago. One of the most obvious *other* services that an automobile *may* provide is snob appeal. That flashy pile of chrome and acrylic enamel can be a very important status symbol for some people. You may think this is wrong, but who are you to say so? If you allow free choice, the other guy's tastes are his own business. You may laugh at his choice but that won't make him "wrong" and you "right" unless you carry a very large stick and thus somehow convince him that his tastes are foolish.

Even the quality of the transportation service itself may vary considerably. Will you accept a cold, bumpy ride to the local emporium or do you insist on cushioned comfort for the trip? There are also many other "intangible" characteristics in the services that flow from any commodity. For example, I have a colleague who is obviously out of his tree (in my opinion, of course). He spends great quantities of money buying a particular foreign car that is (1) small, (2) expensive to maintain, (3) not terribly handsome, and (4) hard to get serviced. Why would anyone act this way? In this case, the answer lies in the fact that the car is truly a mechanical jewel. My friend derives considerable pleasure from just owning and operating this mechanical masterpiece. In fact, the enjoyment is sufficiently great to induce him to *pay* resources and buying power well in excess of those which would be required for transportation services alone. Mind you, this pleasure is not (just) to impress his friends and neighbors. He truly derives satisfaction in having the use of such a fine piece of equipment. Therefore, according to our *earlier* discussion, his purchase of this kind of automobile is perfectly *rational*.

Still another example. I am an absolute nut about sailing—you know sailing, with *sail-boats,* not those noisy worthless floating egg crates called powerboats. This is bad enough in many people's eyes, (particularly to my long-suffering wife), but to add insult to injury, I like *wooden* sailboats—not those miserable plastic palaces that tend to look like hatboxes on rafts. A wooden sailboat (1) is generally slower, (2) is much more expensive to maintain, (3) tends to fall apart from dry rot, and (4) loses value like a leaking money sack. Why do I put up with (and pay for) such problems? Because, *to me* this is the only proper kind of vessel and is, therefore, a rational purchase.

There is another kind of service that certain goods can provide. Some of my more "liberal" (in the twentieth-century sense of the term) friends wouldn't be caught dead in any automobile bigger or better than a 1950 VW. It would destroy their whole image as respectably undernourished intellectuals. In this case, the *lack* of a certain flow of service from the commodity actually provides a *positive* benefit to the owner. Ah well, it's a nutty world, but we might as well admit it and get on with the business of muddling through.

All right, then, to recap: all goods have value because and *only* because of the services which holders of the goods derive. These services can be many and varied for a single good. The services can also be very different for different people. The amount of resources and/or buying power that a person will be willing to give up is a function of (depends upon) the value of the services *as viewed by the buyer*.

We're beginning to get at some of the real basics of economics and the economic problem. Starting with the concept of scarcity, we have seen that scarcity is really *created* by man's wanting more of the services of particular goods than can be made available without his giving up something else. This situation lays the groundwork for big problems. If there is more than one person wanting the same item, who's going to get it and under what conditions? The answer to this particular question will depend on the kind of economic system that the community employs. But before this problem can even be considered, it is necessary to bring in another concept—the idea of property.

The whole business of *property* really boils down to a bundle of *rights* connected with some tangible thing *or* the services flowing from some tangible thing. *Property rights* to something include the rights to *use*, to *prevent use*, to *transfer to others*, and to *destroy* the item in question. Clearly, as long as something isn't *scarce*, the whole question of property is either irrelevant or, at most, not very important. But if something is scarce, then the whole idea and definition of property and the rights associated with property become essential. No system can even begin the solution of the scarcity problem until such rights are defined, established, and enforced. From the standpoint of *economic efficiency alone*, this definition, establishment, and enforcement is much more important than the other question of who gets the rights and under what conditions. Again, a simple example may help.

Imagine that as of noon tomorrow, the several governments under which we live announce that property rights to automobiles will no longer exist. All laws that protect the right of an individual to "own" an automobile will be null and void. Stealing an automobile will no longer be illegal. Instead, it will be illegal for anyone to try and maintain any individual right to some particular car. One very important point must be kept in mind. Today, while property rights still exist, and before we were told that the rights were about to disappear, getting the rights to use a car involved giving up some other resource. In other words, cars were *scarce* because there were not enough to go around on a free basis. Remember, too, that when the announcement removing property rights on cars was made, the announcement said *removal* of property rights—not just transfer of those rights to some government (expropriation) or to some other authoritarian group. Rights are to be just plain *eliminated*. With very little imagination one can easily predict what would happen following noon tomorrow. If you owned a car, you no longer would own a car—nobody would own a car. Anyone could grab your car and use it to his heart's content. You couldn't do anything to stop him. If you *tried* to stop him, you'd be wrong and subject to legal action. By the same token, there would be nothing stopping you from grabbing someone else's (formerly) car and using it for your own purposes. Of course, since no one would have to pay for using cars anymore, there would be an immediate shortage, and this shortage would probably be solved by people grabbing on a first-come, first-served basis. In such a situation, the importance to individuals of having the services of an auto available will no longer be reflected in the amount of alternative goods they are willing and able to pay to get such services. The market will no longer ration the scarce items because the market no longer has anything to allocate. Without defined property rights, there can be no transaction.

This removal of property rights will also have some longer-run effects that will be disastrous, unless you think getting rid of the automobile completely is a good idea. First of all, who is going to maintain the existing stock of autos in some kind of running order? I might be willing to patch up some old bucket to get me from here to there one time, but I certainly am not going to spend any of my resources on proper maintenance, since it will merely benefit the next guy who grabs the car. Clearly, the existing stock will deteriorate in a hurry, and, of course, it's *very* unlikely that any new cars will replace the ones that are wearing out. Who's going to buy new cars? You can bet I'm not going to lay out two or three grand for a car that can be grabbed by the first person who sees it. The point is that there really is nothing to buy! It is the property rights over a good from which services can be derived. It is these rights that are actually exchanged in market transactions. When these property rights are (1) ill-defined, (2) non-existent, (3) unenforced, or (4) incomplete, no allocation system in the world will succeed in allocating the goods concerned in any orderly or rational way.

Again, and again, and still again, it is the property rights that are exchanged in any market process. You never "buy a good." What you do buy is a bundle of property rights associated with that good that will entitle you to obtain certain services from it. Some years ago, Richard Burton bought a king-sized diamond for Liz Taylor. I don't think many people really know for sure just what the price was, but it was plenty. What did he really purchase? For one thing, lots of snob appeal. For another thing, it could be a very expensive glass-cutter. The rights that he purchased are very general indeed. If he wished to destroy the diamond, the law would let him. If he wished to sell the diamond (that is, the property rights associated with the diamond) to someone else, the law would allow him to do so, and would even enforce the rights thus transferred. If he wanted to break the thing into smaller pieces, that would be okay. If he doesn't want someone else to use the diamond, the law will support this right as well. Even though *very* general, the rights which Burton has regarding the diamond are still not absolute. For example, it would be illegal for him to use the diamond as a missile to clobber some critic. It would be illegal for him to use the rock to cut up plate glass windows on Fifth Avenue. Even the most general sale of property rights generally has some kinds of restrictions against completely indiscriminate use of the good. This is particularly true if such indiscriminate use might infringe on someone else's rights.

Does all this mean that property rights must be vested in individuals in order to have an economic system? Of course not. The choice of who will hold what property rights generally involves decisions as to what people think is "right" and "wrong." If you believe in a large measure of individual freedom of action, then in all probability you will advocate a system of private individual property. On the other hand, if you feel that the community should exercise substantial control over goods and services, you will probably advocate a large measure of state ownership and control of goods and services. The most important point to remember, however, is that this decision of who should get the rights *is independent* of the proposition that rights must exist and be enforced.

It is interesting that today there are groups which would like to "tear down the establishment." Apparently these groups exist in both controlled and "free" economies. Given the goal of destroying the existing order, whatever it is, the tactic of debasing the law, destroying *any* property right structure, and dismissing any evolutionary systematic change is very well conceived. If you want to get at the guts of any society, undermine its system of property rights and rights enforcement. The course of action doesn't solve any problems, but it is a good way to kill the old—good or bad.

Questions and Problems for Chapter 2

1. Consider some major purchase that you have made or that has been made for you in your lifetime. List all the services which you derived (or hope to derive) from that commodity. Could this item have been rented instead of purchased? Why did you buy instead of rent? Would the services from the item have been different if you had rented it?

2. List the differences between your property rights to the classroom you occupy and the home in which you live.

3. Why do you see more beer cans and trash along highway right-of-ways than on suburban lawns?

4. If cars became a "free good," as described in the example in this chapter, would you expect more pollution from exhaust fumes? Why?

5.   Assume that all of the countries in Africa declared that anyone could lay claim to any diamond he could find in the many diamond areas. The existing companies (which hold a virtual monopoly on diamond mining and marketing) would no longer be able to enforce their rights in the mining property. What do you think would happen? How about the value of Liz Burton's giant rock?

6.   In some places, it is possible to buy stolen goods for prices considerably cheaper than would normally be charged in legal markets. Why is this so?

7.   You buy a piece of land and the owner insists on a clause that says *he* still keeps the right to say who *you* might resell the property to in the future. Would this clause tend to increase or decrease the price of the land? Why?

8.   Is a 1930 Chevrolet auto the same good as a 1972 Chevrolet? Why or why not?

9.   As violence in inner-city areas increased in recent years, the cost of goods purchased from inner-city stores tended to rise. Explain.

10.   "A man who buys a car to use in his business has an economic reason for doing so. The car he buys for his wife to use for social functions is purchased for non-economic reasons." Comment on these statements.

3. The Market Idea — Exchange and Money

Just look at how much you've learned so far! People don't buy goods. Goods have value only because of the services they yield to man. Property rights must exist for any scarce good if allocation is to be carried out in any systematic way. Whether you realize it or not, just understanding these simple facts puts you ahead of many people who claim to be professional economists.

Just how do these property rights get transferred from one person or entity to another person or entity? There are several ways this can take place. As has already been implied, the community can set up some kind of ruling body and empower it to make any and all decisions about goods and services. Whatever system we come up with must answer these basic issues:

1. Given the stock of *scarce* goods, the wealth that is available right now, how are we going to ration them among the number of people that want them? (Remember, we're talking about *scarce* goods. There aren't enough to go around *on a free basis* to all those who would like some *on a free basis*).

2. How are we going to produce more goods in the future? Who is going to be employed in what occupation? What machine is going to be used to produce which good?

3. What are we going to produce? Should all the community's efforts be directed toward producing factories and other machines for greater future productivity, or should goods and services that consumers like be made now? Will it be punch-presses or refrigerators, power dams or hair dryers?

4. Finally, the billion dollar question must be answered, and this one causes more

fights than any of the others. Who is going to get how much of the pie? Should everyone receive the same income regardless of their productivity? Should people be rewarded according to the value of their product to "society"? By the way, what is "society"? Again, this is the area where value judgments reign and where right or wrong does not exist except in people's minds.

Clearly, it should be possible for our ruling group to answer these questions in some manner or other. There are several alternatives available to solve the rationing bit. One of the most common ways of handling shortages is to use the good old queue. If you want the thing, line up. First one in line gets the prize. The more you want it, the more willing you will be to give up *time* standing in line. Another way to ration the goods is to let everyone fight over them. This way, the strongest get the goods and the weakest lose out. Although you may not think it fair, it's one of the oldest laws going and it does perform the rationing function. Still another method is to have the friends and relatives of the ruling group take all the goods and to heck with the rest of the community. Unfair? It depends on your point of view. If you're one of the ruling elite, chances are you'll think things are just fine; but if you're one of the peons, your attitude may be slightly different. Finally, you might decide to set up some other kind of criteria for allocating the scarce goods. For example, if milk is particularly short, you may decide that families with very small children should receive the limited supply available. You could probably set up whole volumes of rules and regulations to govern the distribution of each and every item that needs to be rationed. It would be very cumbersome, but this sort of approach *could* handle the basic rationing problem.

There could be one other way of solving the many problems that are lumped together as "economic." If men would only live in isolation and keep out of each other's hair, many (though not all) of the economic problems would be taken care of in at least one sense. All those disputes over *exchange* and *trade* would be eliminated because trade and exchange would be eliminated. Why don't we solve the problem of fighting between men in just this way? After all, most of the serious feuds and wars are caused by some scarcity issue, which interchange between men seems to generate. If we were to go back to the simple pastoral life in which everyone did everything necessary for his existence, we wouldn't need the feud-generating phenomenon of trade.

This is not likely to occur because almost all men want more than they can produce with their own capabilities. Not all men are created equal, with all due deference to Mr. Jefferson. As someone said, "Some are created more equal than others." This is particularly true with respect to abilities in producing different goods and services. Whatever the differences in men at their creation, differences in productive skills become even greater as they mature. Whatever the reasons, men do possess different abilities in producing different commodities. This simple fact leads inescapably to the primary reason for economic intercourse. Men can gain more for themselves *and potentially for their community as well* by specializing in the skills which they can do *relatively* or *comparatively* best. Of course, if men are going to specialize, this probably means that they won't have time to produce the variety of goods that they want for their own livelihood. In order for specialization to make any sense at all, trade must take place. The excess of the specialty production of one man can be traded for the excess specialty production of another man. Both men *potentially* can gain from this process. Who is going to gain the most is another question, which will be considered later in more detail. At this point, however, the important idea is that man's wants lead him to seek better ways of producing more goods, which in turn yield him satisfying services. This search has caused him to do his *thing* rather than to do his *things*. When everyone in a community does this, it is possible to exchange each trader's surplus to the mutual benefit of all. But for the gain to be meaningful, *trade or exchange must take place.* This may sound like a bunch of capitalist propaganda, but the truth of this statement is just as valid for Mao's China or Castro's Cuba as it is for the United States or Great Britain. The difference between these economic systems is not the need for trade, but rather how that trade is to be carried out. How are the four functions of an economic system to be implemented? As has already been indicated, there are at least three basic ways these functions can be carried out *in addition* to the way that will be discussed in most detail in this book. They are:

1. Rule and decision-making by the law of the strongest.
2. Rule and decision by a traditional elite.
3. Rule and decision by an elected or appointed elite.

Clearly, many systems will combine elements of each of these three possibilities; and, almost always, the systems will employ another method as well—the market.

The market, in its broadest sense, merely refers to some kind of interaction between people who have something to *sell*, that is, something in excess of their immediate wants, and other people who desire the "something" in question. In the absence of force or coercion, these buyers and sellers dicker back and forth until a *price* is arrived at which will (1) entice the seller to sell and (2) entice the buyer to buy. This is a simpleminded concept, but its ramifications can and do fill volumes. In this volume, however, we'll concentrate on some of the more important aspects of markets as they affect your daily lives.

While it would be out of order in most consumer economics textbooks, I want first to discuss a good which is essential to the *efficient* operation of any market system—that is, any complex market system involving production above subsistence levels. The good in question is *money*. Most of you have probably never looked on money as being a good, but it most assuredly is. Remember, we said that a good is something from which we derive services, and an economic good is one which is scarce in addition to yielding services. So it is with money. The services yielded by money are probably among the least recognized of any good. We really take it for granted. True, we all want more of it and are willing to work in order to get more, but why? Except for the miser who gains pleasure from just hoarding money, this crazy commodity doesn't have any "intrinsic" value, no value in itself. For that matter, nothing has any value in itself. *Man* gives any good its value. Value is a man-made concept. So why is money "valuable"? Obviously, because of the goods and services which can be obtained by *exchanging* money for them. The value of money rests exclusively on its ability to purchase things now and/or in the future. True, money is used for purposes other than exchange, or as the economist would put it, a medium of exchange. But basically, money's value *as money* rests upon its exchange value.

Wouldn't the world really be better off without money? Like the question of eliminating trade, this question deserves a serious answer, particularly since so many people today seem to feel that "Money is the root of all evil." As in a world without trade, finding an example of a world without money of some sort is virtually impossible. You're going to have to use your imagination and stretch it to the limit. Assume that tomorrow morning you wake up and turn on the TV for the morning news. The lead story consists of an announcement by the president that money in any form whatsoever is illegal and anyone trying to set up any money system will be liable for the death penalty. Use of money has become a capital offense. (Sorry about that.) Thank God, say all the anti-money types. Now the world will rid itself of all evil and life can become pure and simple. As you go about your morning routine, nothing seems to have changed. The same old life and the same old routine. It's payday and you go to work happy in the thought that today you can reap the fruits of your past two-weeks labor. Lunchtime comes and goes, and still there is no apparent change in your life style. The brown-bag lunch you prepared is the same as always. Now for the glorious moment—payday. Your job is operating a machine that makes nuts and bolts. Push one button and out comes a nut; push the other button and out comes a bolt. Those nuts and bolts are the fruit of your labor, so guess what! That's what you're going to be paid—nuts and bolts. The springs on the old muscle car sag under the load, but you take your pay home to figure out the next step. Really, it's easy. You have a friend working in another factory down the street, and that factory uses the kind of nuts and bolts you were paid in. All that need be done is to sell the nuts and bolts to the factory, and your troubles are over. Just a minute. No more money, remember? That factory makes chrome-plated coat racks, and your need for chrome-plated coat racks just isn't very great. However, maybe you can trade *some* of your nuts and bolts for a few coat racks, and then you might be able to trade some of the coat racks to the local supermarket for a few groceries. Better yet, since the supermarket employees are now being paid in groceries (if they're lucky), maybe the check-out girl would like to trade some groceries for a coat rack. This example is *not* ridiculous! Without money, you would have to be paid with your own production. You would then have to find somebody else who wanted what you produced. Worse than that, you would have to find someone who wanted your product *and had something you wanted*. Obviously, everyone would end up spending 99.9 percent of his waking hours arranging various exchanges and .1 percent of his time actually working. The end results would most certainly be the destruction of productive society as we know it. Modern industry and the gains resulting from specialization would disappear. Trade would become so expensive that only the simplest kinds of barter would be worthwhile. We would be forced back into a prehistoric economic world.

You think this is overstating the case? Not at all. Money is the most important good in any modern economy, be it "capitalistic" or "socialistic." Its value comes into being because of its ability to facilitate transactions between presently-available goods and goods that will become available in the future.

Think about this last point for a moment. If you were paid in nuts and bolts, you could hold some of these items to spend on your future needs. This future might be a short as tonight's dinner or as long term as a nest egg for your great-grandson's college education. You would use the fruits of your *present* productivity to store purchasing power for future demands. Nuts and bolts might work for this purpose, but you would be in serious trouble if you were a fisherman or a milk producer.

Money has, therefore, two basic general uses. It serves to facilitate transactions at any moment in time, and it allows "storage" of current purchasing power so that it can procure other goods at some future time. People's *demand* for money results from these two valuable uses of money.

Most goods continue to yield some services even through they become comparatively abundant. Money is perverse in this respect. An excess of money can actually decrease the services yielded by all units, even the first ones issued. Drinking water fulfills a bodily need. Even if we're flooded with drinking water, its ability to satisfy that bodily need is not diminished. An excess of money, on the other hand, can destroy the usefulness of all units of money. As we show how that occurs, you should begin to see how something called inflation works. By now, you should be accustomed to using your imagination to create an *abstract* simple situation to help understand the workings of a *concrete*, complicated real world.

Assume that the class you're in is suddenly transported to the nearest supermarket shopping complex. This complex contains all the goods that you and your classmates might want and have the ability to purchase. In other words, if you all spend all the money you have, the total amount will come to exactly the value of the goods in the complex. The stores will end up with all your money and you'll end up with all their goods. This is really a stroke of luck since you and your friends actually had the chance to bid among yourselves for the available goods, and the resulting prices cleared the stores of all their goods—no more and no less. Now let's repeat the operation.

Assume that everything stays the same, including all of your individual and collective desires for the goods. The stores are restocked in exactly the same way, and no goods can be added or subtracted from the shelves once you get in the complex. We will allow one difference, however. We'll allow an airplane to fly over the complex and drop dollar bills down on you and your friends in such a way that *each* of you now has exactly twice as many dollars as you had before. Armed with this bonanza in buying power you all start the bidding and trading process over again. This time we won't let any sale become final until all bids have been offered and taken. What do you think the outcome will be? Before, you were willing and able to pay $1.00 for a pair of socks. Now you've got twice as much buying power, so you try to buy more of everything, including socks. (You wouldn't necessarily try to buy twice as many pairs of socks. This might or might not be the case and is not a necessary part of the argument at this time.) The problem is that you're not the only one with twice as much buying power.

Everyone now has twice as much buying power and yet there is only as much to buy as there was before. So you all start bidding with one another, and up go the money prices. How far up will they go? Under the strict conditions we have imposed on our abstract model, they will exactly double. Would this happen in the real world? If the available goods and services were *fixed*, and the money supply was *doubled*, and markets were operating in a free and knowledgeable fashion, this is precisely what would happen!

Let's look at the above situation in terms of the "set theory" developed earlier. In Figure 3.1a, we show the equivalent of the "utopia" described in Chapter 1. Of course, it isn't utopia for everyone involved in the market, but it is utopian in that people's desires *and abilities in terms of purchasing power* are equal in magnitude to the satisfiers (goods and services) available. The market is said to be in equilibrium. There are plenty of desires of the demanders left unsatisfied but, given their *buying power*, they are satisfied to exactly the extent of the available goods. To show the function of money we have assumed a fixed stock of satisfiers. However, over time, this stock can change.

In Figure 3.1b, we have doubled the apparent purchasing power by doubling the available money supply. Our desires and *apparent* abilities to purchase have doubled but, again, the available goods remain constant. The "utopian" equilibrium has been disturbed and there is an excess of desires and apparent abilities to purchase—excess in that there are no more goods to be had. What happens has already been covered. *Prices* will go up so that with *twice* the money supply, the price of each and every good in the satisfier group will go to *twice* its former level. The apparent purchasing power of the increased money supply has been cut in half so that twice the original quantity of money will buy *exactly the same* quantity of goods and services. Figure 3.1c shows this purchasing power collapsing back to the same level it originally had—equal to the available goods.

Since this *price* business is obviously very important indeed, a word or two more at this juncture might be a good idea. You all understand the *dollar price* of goods. This is a concept that you use every day. The dollar price of anything is the number of dollars (or fraction of dollars) that you must *give up* in order to get *one unit* of the good in question. Coffee is 15/100 of one dollar ($.15) *per cup*. An automobile of some specific set of specifications costs 3,000 dollars *per car*. However, you don't need money in order to talk about price. The price of *anything* is whatever must be given up of something else to get one unit of the good in question. If you marry Ethel (or George), the cost (in addition to the money cost) of marrying Ethel may be giving up dates with Clementine. One marriage to Ethel *costs*, say, one hundred dates with Clementine. The Clementine-dates *price* of marriage was 100 dates *per marriage*. In countries which still allow this sort of thing, the price of one wife might be 10 camels *per wife*.

Figure 3.1
Equilibrium and Satisfiers

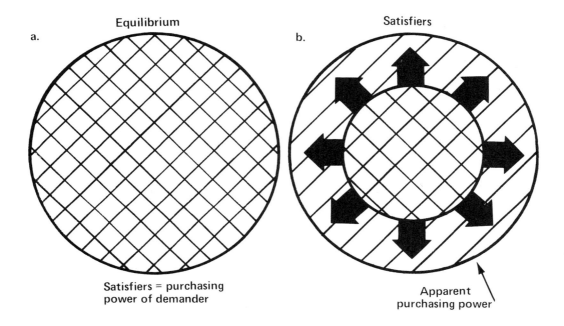

Equilibrium

a.

Satisfiers = purchasing
power of demander

Satisfiers

b.

Apparent
purchasing power

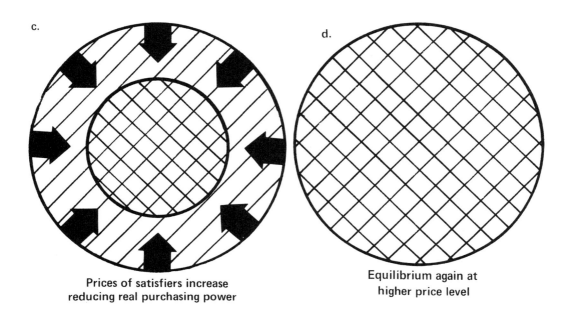

c.

Prices of satisfiers increase
reducing real purchasing power

d.

Equilibrium again at
higher price level

In any *barter* arrangement which does not use money, prices are expensive in terms of the amount of one good that must be *paid* (given up) in order to get one unit of the other good.

One price you have probably never thought about is the *price of dollars*. What is the price of having and using money? Your friendly banker will tell you that the price of money equals the amount of interest you must pay to borrow a dollar. He's partially right, but he's talking about the price of money that's being *borrowed*, not the price of whatever stock of money exists to carry out current transactions. Remember, we have defined the price of anything as being that which must be given up to get one unit of the good in question. If you buy *a* book for $10.00, the price of the book is $10.00. If books are the only thing you're using money to purchase, then it's very easy to find the price of money. In this case, the *price* of *getting* or *holding* one dollar would be *not* getting or holding 1/10 of one book. Okay, I know that you can't generally split books into tenths, but, nevertheless, 1/10 of one book is the price of one dollar. If you're using dollars to purchase many different things, how can you determine the price of one dollar? It's conceptually very simple, although to calculate it you'd have to have fantastic market information and enormous computers. Figure out what goods you and/or your friends buy *on the average* in some particular time period. Call that average bundle of goods a "market basket." Next, calculate the dollar value of that market basket—one market basket costs so many dollars. Now it's simple. If one market basket costs, say, $1,000; then the price of one dollar would be giving up 1/1000 of a market basket. Notice, as the price of market baskets (the goods you buy) goes *up* this is the same thing as saying that the price or *purchasing power* of money goes *down*. In the same way, if the price of market baskets goes *down*, this is the same thing as saying that the price (purchasing power) of dollars goes *up*. Most of you have probably already figured it out, but here we have the basic concepts needed to look at such problems as inflation in the economy.

We also have discussed enough about the functions of money to make it possible to investigate just how markets operate. This is next on the agenda. We'll look at markets involving choices between *current* goods, and then we'll look at the markets involved in making choices of current goods versus future goods. Finally, the operation of the economy as a whole will be discussed briefly, as will be your specific part in the overall economic operation.

Questions and Problems for Chapter 3

1. List events in your own life that have been controlled or substantially influenced by:
   a. some person or group controlling through strength and brute force
   b. a traditional ruling person or body
   c. an elected or appointed ruler
   d. a "free" market

2. How did your personal freedom fit into each of the situations listed above?

3.   List some instances in which something you considered scarce was rationed at least in part by "queuing." If the *other* costs of obtaining the good in question had been higher, what would you expect to have happened to the size of the queue?

4.   Take a dollar bill from your pocket. What does the producer of that bill promise to do? What are the potential things you could do or get with that bill besides goods and services?

5. Most of you probably have done some kind of do-it-yourself project. Why did you do this project? There are other types of do-it-yourself projects that you are probably *capable* of performing. Why don't you do them?

6. Discuss the statement "Money is the root of all evil."

7.   Compare the advantages and disadvantages of using different things to store value. Some examples are harem wives, wheat, a checking account, a savings account, an investment in the stock market, a new car, cash money.

8.   List all the non-money prices you have had to face or estimate in the recent past. Remember, *price* is the *per unit* cost of something, not merely what you paid out in total.

9.   How is using a credit card similar to using money? What functions can money perform that credit cards can't?

10.   Is there any set of circumstances under which you could produce your own "wants" without relying on the productive abilities of anyone else? What circumstances would come closest to that possibility?

PART TWO
You in the Marketplace — Now

In this section we're going to look at your position in the economy. What this involves is getting you to consider in some depth the way you actually make day-to-day decisions between scarce alternatives. At least ninety percent of the time, you can understand economic theory by simply asking yourself what you would do when faced with the assumed conditions. The other ten percent of the time you might be wrong because people *are* different and behavior that is rational for one person is not always rational for someone else.

Why does anyone do anything? Is there any thread of consistency in people's actions that can be generalized into a useful concept or theory? These two questions are our current subject. In Chapter 1, rationality was described as existing when individuals tried to make their net satisfaction as large as possible. This idea needs considerable expansion. For a long time, economists tried to put numbers on this idea of satisfaction. Instead of calling it "satisfaction," they used the word *utility*. People were said to operate in such a way as to *maximize* their *utility* in life. Some economists even went so far as to suggest a measurable unit of utility—a util. It was said that people took any course of action because the number of utils they gained from the action more than offset the utils they lost from the *cost* of that action.

This idea seemed reasonable until one asked the rather embarrassing question, "How do you actually measure utility?" A lot of the controversy among economists on this measurability business went way out into left field. Most of it would be of little interest to you at this stage of your exposure to economics. But in the process of discussing this problem, most of these economists came to realize that the whole problem of measuring utility in concrete terms wasn't really all that necessary, and a great deal could be said about the decision-making process without having to figure out a single number on someone's "utility scale." All that is essential to the choice between several alternatives is that the chooser be able to *order* his preferences among the alternatives. If I go into a bar and order a drink, I couldn't care less how many utils will be gained by one Scotch-on-the-rocks. I *do* have to care whether one Scotch-on-the-rocks will yield more or less satisfaction or utility than one bourbon-on-the-rocks. Were I seriously considering a bourbon-on-the-rocks, it would also be well to know whether the bourbon was preferable to a stein of beer.

Assuming that the total cost of each alternative was identical, the decision of which alternative to take could be rationally made based solely on the *order* of preference. I'm making one more assumption as well. If the Scotch is preferred to the bourbon, and the bourbon is preferred to the beer, I will assume that the Scotch is also preferred to the beer. Just to impress your friends, this last idea is called *transitivity*. If *A* is preferred to *B*, and *B* is preferred to *C*, then *A* is also preferred to *C*. Notice, our example assumes also that the set of choices available was merely the consumption of one of the three choices mentioned. This says nothing about the choice of entering the bar in the first place, or perhaps having brandy or creme de menthe instead of the listed alternatives. What it *does* say is that whatever the choice set, as long as one can order the preferences of the alternatives within the set, a rational choice of action can be made.

A few key words were sneaked into the previous few paragraphs and, whether or not you noticed them, they need to be discussed. Several times, the phrase *"net satisfaction"* has been used. Also, I said that within our choice set, the *cost* of each alternative was the same. When one talks about something being a *net result*, it means that there are two or more actions operating in different directions. After the effect of each is offset by effects of the others, there is something left over. This "leftover" is the net result. As we discuss alternative courses of action, one can assume that such alternatives will each produce some potential *benefit—* something positive will happen which will be desirable. But if we're talking about alternative actions that each would be desirable (yield utility), then *there is always a cost associated with the alternative*. That may sound like a strong general statement, but it is absolutely true *without exception*. Some of these costs may be very obvious. They may even take the form of *money costs*. But the cost that always exists when alternatives are available is the one called *opportunity cost*. This one needs to be understood if you are really going to make rational choices in your life.

Think of your own situation right this minute. Presumably you are reading this book, or at least attempting to read this book. Are there any other alternative uses for your time right now? I would wager that for almost all of you the answer is a strong *yes*. Some of you might rather be watching TV. Others might rather be taking a bath, or eating, or making love, or even earning money on some job or other. Whatever alternative you actually gave up to read this book at this time—that *foregone alternative*—is a cost of reading the book. It's possible that you have incurred other costs as well. For instance, some of you may have driven to school to find peace and quiet in the library. The costs of getting to and from the library must also be charged up against the benefits expected from reading the book.

What about these benefits? Many of you are probably reading this book because it is required for the course you're taking. Chances are that many of you are even taking the course because it is a requirement for graduation. A few of you may actually be trying to learn something from the course. Whatever the reason or reasons, each of you has weighted the benefits you are getting *now* plus the benefits you expect to get in the future against the total cost of reading *now*. Whatever the mechanics of your reasoning process, the fact that you *are reading* shows that you felt there would be a *net benefit* rather than a *net cost* to the course of action adopted. Again, we can look at this idea in graphical form. Figure 4.1 shows an outer area which represents gross benefits from some course of action, for example, reading this book. Within this set of benefits, ther is another area which represents the costs of reading the book. Remember, these costs include any out-of-pocket expenses that might be incurred as well as the costs of foregone alternatives. As long as the benefits area exceeds the costs area, you will read. Should the opposite be true—should costs exceed benefits—you would presumably do something else. Notice something interesting in this diagram (and analysis). Sure, you're interested in the size of the total benefits, but your primary interest is in the size of the *net* benefits. Graphically, you will attempt to make the "rim" outside the cost area and inside the benefits area as large as possible. This can be done by *either* doing something that makes the benefit area larger *or* by doing something that makes the cost area smaller *or* some combination of both things. This is obvious, but many times events tend to be viewed from their benefit *or* cost side *only*, rather than from the "net" concept of benefits, viewed in the context of their corresponding costs.

When it comes to making decisions ragarding many alternatives in many different areas, the operation is the same. Consciously or unconsciously, benefits and costs are added together. Whether or not an additional possible action is taken will depend upon whether doing it will *add* to the net benefits or detract from net benefits. Figure 4.2 illustrates the point. Existing actions show a bundle of benefits or expected benefits greater than costs or expected costs. In the upper left-hand corner of the figure, another possible action is shown. Since the person expects this action to yield more benefits than costs, he will take the action. The benefits of this act will add to the existing benefits and the cost will be added to the existing costs. *Net* benefits of the new bundle of actions will be increased. On the other hand, a possible action such as illustrated in the lower left-hand corner would not be undertaken since more costs than benefits would be added to the present package.

This may seem like a tremendous amount of effort to explain a completely simpleminded principle but, hopefully, it will help you remember at all times the relationship between benefits (broadly defined) and costs (broadly defined) in making decisions between available alternative choices. The behavior just described can be called *maximizing behavior*. To some

Figure 4.1
Cost/Benefits of Reading

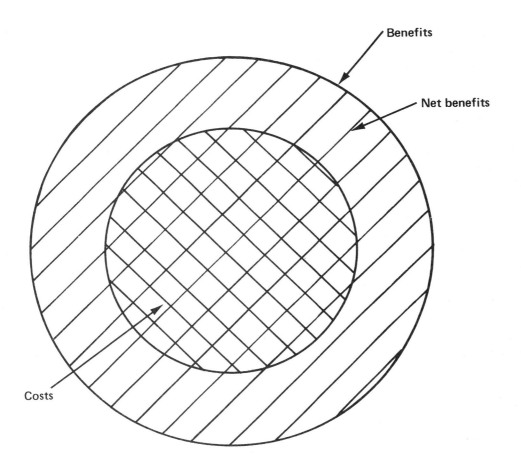

Figure 4.2

Possible action No. 1

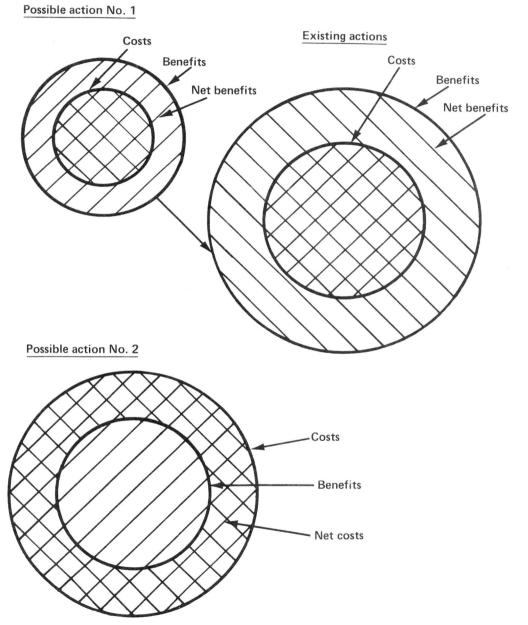

Existing actions

Costs

Benefits

Net benefits

Costs

Benefits

Net benefits

Possible action No. 2

Costs

Benefits

Net costs

people, the word *maximizing* implies that things can be actually measured. To avoid this misunderstanding, the word *optimizing* seems more appropriate. Take your pick. As long as you see what's going on, the words are relatively unimportant. The point, however, is anything but trivial. Men generally act in such a way as to optimize their total happiness, utility, satisfaction, well-being, welfare, contentment or what have you. This merely means that they will undertake actions which they think or expect will add more to this benefit package than it will detract. Obviously, this doesn't mean that net benefits *right now* have to become greater. Were this the case, nobody would ever save anything. We would all live precisely for this moment as though there were to be no future. All of the cost/benefits are really *expected* cost benefits. There is little absolute certainty in this world (even death and taxes are less than *completely* certain). Expectations guide our every move and some of the concrete results of this will be looked at later in the book.

I'm sure some of you who have read the preceding pages are concerned about the philosophical implications of rational behavior therein described. "My God," say you, "what you're saying is that man is basically selfish and all his actions are based solely on increasing his own happiness." It really isn't quite that bad. You see, we haven't ruled out "unselfishness" as one possible benefit to our behavior. Some people gain tremendous psychic (or spiritual) benefits from helping others. They will help others at costs to themselves (again, as long as the perceived benefits exceed the perceived costs). Don't make the mistake of assuming economic behavior must apply *only* to material things nor that self-satisfying behaviour must necessarily take the form of imposing costs on others. This doesn't have to be the case. It is true that much of the upcoming discussion will primarily concern man's quest for greater material prosperity. We will be assuming that man generally would prefer *more* material goods than less. That doesn't mean he will always want more of any one good, but that, in total he will prefer more rather than less.

So far, the title of this chapter doesn't make any sense. The caption implies that each of us tries to act like a *single seller of something* (that's what monopolist means). In a way, this is just what most people try to do. Our optimizing behavior results in our trying to get just as much as we can for as little cost as possible. None of us much likes the idea of someone else coming into our territory. In everyday life, nobody (at least nobody in a union) likes the idea of a "scab" coming into a factory to do a given job at a lower wage than he is getting. We all have individual ideas of what our product is worth, and most often this amount is larger than the amount we can actually get in the marketplace. There always seems to be someone who is willing (and able) to undercut the obviously "fair" price we should get for our product, be the product a good or the services of our labor. This competition in our material lives seems to be an absolute pain in the neck. Yet it is the same competition that provides one of the counterbalances to purely selfish behavior that, by itself, might be inefficient. This statement probably doesn't make a great deal of sense at this stage, but let it form the watchword for the upcoming chapter on production. Here we can see how each of us would-be monopolists actually performs in the material world.

Questions and Problems for Chapter 4

1. Think about the various alternatives you have for activities next weekend. Take the time to list these alternatives. What are the costs, money and otherwise, of each alternative? How much satisfaction would each activity yield? How do *you* estimate the satisfaction you expect?

2. Place *alternative* activities in the order you would prefer if cost were the same for each. Obviously, you will be able to carry out several different activities, so rank only *alternatives*. Now order the activities considering the estimated costs involved. Is there any difference in the two orderings? If so, how come?

3.   In the problem above, did you remember to count as cost the satisfaction or utility you could have gained from the *foregone alternative*?

4.   If you want to go one step in a given direction, and do so using your left foot, what is the alternative cost? Without jumping or leaping, what happens when you try to step with both feet at the same time? The same thing happens in a figurative sense whenever actions are taken that ignore scarcity or limits.

5.   How do you maximize net benefits from your own study program? What do you consider the cost and benefits? How many of these can be measured in dollars and cents now? Will this measurement change in the future?

6.   Explain the fact that some people perform work for a charitable organization "for free," that is, without receiving wages equal to their usual working wage. List possible costs and benefits in this kind of action.

7. Explain the effects of law and law enforcement on the behavior of individuals in a society. Using Venn diagrams, show what is being attempted when judges impose more severe sentences for illegal acts.

8. Do you consciously weigh the costs and benefits of every action you take? Why don't you do this? Decision-making itself involves costs.

9. Consider your program for next summer's vacation. Assuming you have already decided what you will be doing, analyze the costs and benefits, including opportunity costs.

10. Does the opportunity cost of your time change during different times of the day? How do these changes affect the different activities you carry out at different times of the day?

5. Producing Stuff

Did you ever ask yourself what "producing" really means? Like so many other words that we use casually, the real meaning and implications are seldom analyzed. Producing, or the concept of production, is merely the utilization of one thing (or a combination of things) to make something else. Things that go into the production process are called *inputs* and whatever comes out on the other end are *outputs*.

Why do we produce anything at all? The answer is that material goods and services *can* contribute to that idea of utility or satisfaction that was discussed in the last chapter. The moment man used his hand to move food from a leafy plant into his mouth, production of sorts took place. In this primitive example, the output was the "service" of moving food from plant to mouth. In an economy without tools or techniques, production generally consists of this type of activity. Man grubs along to keep alive, and if the environment around him is at all harsh, the chances are that he won't survive very long. The *direct* product of man's hands alone is very limited. Of course, even primitive man discovered at an early point in history that he could use part of his time to produce things which couldn't be used *directly* but which could improve his "productivity" over the long run. These things were *tools*—capital goods which were used to improve the productive potential of his own hands and physical efforts. The tool may have been as simple as a convenient-sized rock which could be hurled at the Ice-Age equivalent of a jackrabbit.

Later, rocks were shaped into specialized kinds of tools that could be used for pounding, cutting, scraping or throwing. But none of these rocks were useful in *direct* consumption; their value lay in their capacity to improve the production of something else that *was* useful in consumption. I can see it now. Old Charlie probably spent half a day chipping a particular stone into a spearhead. Old Charlie's unliberated wife probably chipped at him incessantly to quit wasting his time and go out and kill tonight's supper. But old Charlie had the idea that half a day spent making the spearhead would save him many hours of hunting with just a throwing rock. Therefore, he continued building up his "capital" in spite of the nagging wife.

Back to the question of why we produce. Man produces things so that he may *consume* them. The ultimate end of all production activities is consumption. True, there may be a lot of intermediate steps and products, but in the end, production is useless unless man uses the product. Even a work of art is made to be "consumed" in the sense that viewing or hearing it provides a "service" to the beholder or listener. It is not consumed in the sense that it is destroyed in the consumption process but, nevertheless, its existence provides a useful service to someone. Factories, machine tools, and even agricultural enterprises may not produce items for immediate consumption. The goods they produce may only be used to make one or a chain of other goods. Ultimately, however, something will result which will be consumed by some-one, sometime.

While we're still talking about the "why" of production, let's return to the briefly mentioned business of specialization. In Chapter 3, the statement was made that people special-ize in order to increase their productivity. This is merely the idea that each person, or group of persons, does the things that he or they can do best. By specializing, they give up the indepen-dence of producing *all* their respective wants, each by himself. If a person is absolutely the best at doing some particular thing, this whole idea is obvious. If I can make spearheads better than anyone else in the world, and you can make spearshafts better than anyone else in the world, it is clear we both could be better off by specializing in our respective things, and trading the excess of our own needs. (However, we wouldn't be in very good shape if no one wanted spears, and the whole concept of "demand" will be considered later.)

Gains from specialization result primarily from opportunity costs. There it is again, *opportunity costs*. I will trade spearheads for spearshafts *because* in terms of what it would cost me (in time or other inputs), I can get more spearshafts through trade than I could by taking my production resources and devoting them to spearshaft making. Again, this is fairly obvious if you think about it for a minute. But there is an even more important point that may *not* be so obvious. This advantage that I have in producing spearheads doesn't have to be absolute as far as the rest of the world, or even as far as the rest of the world with which I might trade. In fact, I could be the world's worst in the production of both spearheads and spearshafts, but as long as my costs of producing one item *in terms of my production alternatives* are less than my potential trading partner's costs *in terms of his production alternatives*, one or both of us can still gain from specialization in the items in which we have *comparative advantages* in produc-tion. I'm not interested in whether or not my partner can produce something "cheaply" or not. I'm interested in what it would cost me if I had to produce the item myself. What would it cost me in other goods and services (perhaps expressed through money) or in my time (again, perhaps expressed through the money value of my services)?

There is an old example, often quoted in economics textbooks, that still demonstrates very well the principle of comparative advantage. A man by the name of Billy Rose was a very fine impresario. In this field, there may have been people with greater ability, but not many. At the same time, Mr. Rose was also the world champion typist. He literally could out-type anyone in the world (or at least anyone willing and able to compete). In other words, Mr. Rose had an absolute advantage both in being an impresario and at typing. Guess what! He still hired typists to do the typing generated by his several endeavors. Think about this one for a minute and you'll see that this is what would be expected. The time that Rose would have had to give up to do his own typing, *even though he was the best typist around*, had much more value when used in his occupation as an impresario. Sure, this difference was expressed through markets using money as a medium of exchange. He "sold" his time as an impresario, and "bought" the time of the secretaries with some of the proceeds. Notice, though, that what was being traded was, in effect, the alternative uses of his time. He had an *absolute* advantage in both typing and being an impresario. The secretaries all had absolute disadvantages in both typing and being impresarios (presumably). Yet Rose had a *comparative* advantage at being an impresario while the secretaries had a *comparative* advantage (compared to Rose) at being secretaries. Trade could *and did* benefit both parties.

Some of you are probably going to point out some activities that seem to make this whole idea ridiculous. "How come people perform do-it-yourself projects?" say you. In all probability the backyard carpenter isn't nearly as efficient as the pro; and even from the standpoint of comparative advantage it is highly unlikely that the amateur wood-butcher will score well against the craftsman. Why, then, doesn't the amateur work in his specialty a bit more and use his extra earnings to buy the services of the professional? Two factors could cause this not to happen. First of all, the do-it-yourselfer may actually enjoy the work involved. In fact, he may have even *paid* for the privilege of doing so by buying tools, taking a shop course, etc. In many cases, with full knowledge, the hacker will make something that is not as good and costs more than its purchased counterpart. There's nothing irrational about that. The maker is deriving utility from both the services of the good itself and the making of it. A second reason can be the fact that the opportunity costs of the amateur may actually be very low outside of working hours. For example, the university pays me a salary which doesn't change at all if I work two hours a day or twenty. In this situation, I did a lot of do-it-yourself projects. Now, however, I'm also writing books in my "spare time." This has increased the opportunity cost of doing handyman work and, as a result, I've greatly reduced this type of activity in the past few months.

This comparative advantage bit is not just a dry little nicety of economic theory. In this simple fact of life lies most of the reason why *any* trade takes place—trade between people, trade between regions, or trade between countries (more on that in Chapter 15). It also holds one of the bright spots in the so-called "dismal" science of economics. In effect, this principle states that one doesn't have to be *absolutely* the best at something in order to improve his lot. Specialization and trade *can* provide one avenue for improvement in the material prosperity of almost anyone.

Another question besides "Why produce?" is "What will be produced?" In any system, the simple answer is merely, "What is wanted?" plus the equally important qualifier, "What is possible?" In Chapter 7, we're going to cover the subject of *demand*, but a brief word about this concept is in order right now.

The economist, like anyone else, knows that people "want" things. But the economist, unlike *some* other people, realizes that we live in a world of scarcity, which means that the choice of one want-satisfying item may well involve giving up an alternative want-satisfying item. Sure, we all *want* anything and everything that will satisfy our wants. But we *demand* those things which our *resources* allow us to obtain and which we are *willing* to sacrifice those resources to obtain. Demand, as used by the economist, implies both *willingness* and *ability* to obtain. Are we necessarily talking about a free market operation when talking about demand? The answer is an emphatic NO! A free market economy implies that all people have a chance to express willingness and ability through back-and-forth bidding with suppliers of some particular good. In a completely controlled economy, demand still exists. The *expressed* demand may be only that of the ruling group or planning group. Nevertheless, the same questions must be faced. What is possible to get, and what will it cost?

One thing ought to be very familiar by this time. The largest determinant in answering the question of what is to be produced is our old friend, opportunity cost. Again, at a very personal level, what determines the job you actually take? Well, one thing is most certainly your particular set of skills and abilities. How you get these and what the skills cost will be covered in Chapter 11. A second determinant will be how much or little you like the work to be done. This certainly will bear on the wage you insist on receiving. However, even more important than either of these two items, the alternatives you have will bear most heavily on your willingness (and ability) to perform some particular job of work. Remember, once you accept a certain job (production of some service), you are giving up your next-best alternative. "Not necessarily," you say. "I can work one job during the day, and then moonlight another one in the evening." Okay, if this is the case, then you're not talking about an alternative, you're talking about a complementary occupation. Now then, how does this opportunity cost or next-best alternative determine what is to be produced? Very simple. If someone offers you a substantial increase in salary to accept a different job (a job which you would enjoy just as much and which you can in fact perform), then the opportunity cost of that offer will exceed the benefits accrued through your present wage. In this case, you'll move to the new job. Sure, you got a better offer, but this really means that the old job costs too much, given the alternative.

This same principle holds whether you're talking about your own individual job or the production decisions of the Board of Directors of General Motors Corporation. The resource inputs change, of course, but the same idea holds. Those responsible for the production decisions will study the alternatives for which the resources under their control could be used. As you will see a bit later in this chapter, the single focus of their decision will be to make a profit—short- or long-range. But to make this profit they will study their production alternatives—their opportunity costs.

Opportunity costs can be determined by the operation of a free market, but they can just as well be influenced by some decision-making body. The slave-labor camps of Nazi Germany or the forced-labor operation of Siberian development still represent choices for the slaves when faced by alternatives. True, the alternatives to working in these occupations were rather severe, including death or torture, but these alternatives still were viewed by the slaves as choices to their work. While no comparison is intended, the whole business of welfare doles in this country, and most others as well, constitute alternatives to work-provided income. A man working forty hours a week for $75 is rather likely to choose the alternative of $80 per week on the dole. He may not. He may actually prefer the income gained by honest sweat to a handout. On the other side of that coin, a salary of $200 per week may not attract a mother of four children into the labor market if she has to leave her children alone or pay $100 per week for babysitters.

Now that you are all experts in the whys and whats of production, let's look at the "hows." These are inputs. The inputs go into a process, and out of the process comes some output(s). The economist generally calls the inputs "Factors of Production." There are four of these that can be identified:

Labor—Sooner or later, all production involves an input of human labor. It may be "blue-collar," "white-collar," "stiff-collar," or "no-collar," but labor it is. The way we'll use the term it applies equally to the janitor pushing a broom or the comptroller sitting in his paneled office. The latter *may* be providing something else too, but at least part of his function can be considered, "labor."

Capital—It has already been stated that not all goods are made for direct consumption. Some goods are useful in producing other goods. Factory buildings fit this category as do machine tools and even inventories of parts and pieces. Things like this are called capital goods. There is a serious problem with capital goods. They are not *immediately* consumable; but at the same time, making them *did* use scarce resources. Therefore, someone, somewhere, sometime had to give up potential consumption. Someone, somewhere, sometime had to *save*. More on this shortly.

What does the use of capital do? Very simple. Capital improves the productivity of those utilizing it. A man can sweep a few square feet of floor space with his hands in an hour. Give him a little capital, say a broom, and he can sweep a few hundred square feet of floor space in an hour. Give him a sweeping machine, and he may be able to cover all the floors in the building in an hour. Any society that has risen above subsistence levels of material production has become increasingly "capitalistic." All of the highly productive processes known to man involve substantial inputs of capital goods. Regardless of the economic system, including so-called socialist or communist systems, there is an extensive and intensive use of capital, and it's probably here to stay. But capital doesn't just "happen." Capital is created—produced. It is produced from generally scarce resources that therefore are not consumed directly.

Natural Resources—A third factor of production is really a special form of capital. It is called *natural resources*. The reason that this type of capital is sometimes considered separately is that natural resources are *exhaustible*. For example, there is so much petroleum under the earth today. True, it is being created very, very slowly all the time; but for all practical purposes there is a finite limit to its existence. Once it is used up, there isn't any more. Historically, agricultural land has been considered a natural and depletable resource. While it still is in many ways, man has found ways to augment the soil—to transform other products into plant nutrients to build or rebuild agricultural lands. In fact, for a good many years, the interest in natural resources as a separate factor of production waned considerably. Man, with his magnificent ego, began to believe he had conquered depletion by constantly finding alternatives to exhaustible resources. Plastics replaced metals, atomic energy replaced fossil fuels, man-made fertilizers replenished farmlands. But now, another (not new) phenomenon has re-awakened interest in the old natural resource economics. The phenomenon is *pollution*. Suddenly, we are realizing that many of our "free" resources that had been taken for granted were neither *free* nor inexhaustible.

Our flowing resources, that is, flowing air and flowing water have been used as though they were a free good; and as a result, they have been *over*-used as far as their waste disposal capacities are concerned. This problem will be discussed in Chapter 8.

Entrepreneurship—Finally, there is a special category of labor that is often considered separately. Economists have a long French name for it—entrepreneurship. Many of you have probably used the word entrepreneur to describe the businessman who makes millions talking on the telephone to all parts of the world. He is a dashing romantic character to be envied and imitated if at all possible. Well, to the economist, the entrepreneur is a bit more mundane, but his function is most important. The entrepreneur is the person who puts all the other bits and pieces of the production process together. In addition to this function, he also makes the key decisions of what and how much to produce. Without these *functions*, nothing happens to actually make the millions of goods from which the community gets useful services.

When our comparatively free market economy was younger, it was fairly simple to identify entrepreneurs. The man who was running his own business which he started from scratch was an entrepreneur. In many cases, the railroad barons and oil magnates also qualified for the title. In today's massive corporations, entrepreneurs are less easily spotted. Usually, a large company doesn't have *one* man making all the entrepreneurial decisions. These decisions are often made by several different men or, in some cases, by committee. Even in planned economies, the entrepreneurial *functions* must be performed. While most Marxist planning boards would probably shudder at the thought of being considered "entrepreneurs," in fact they are performing the tasks associated with this capitalist concept.

There is one misconception that often occurs regarding entrepreneurs. Just because someone is in "management" does *not* mean that he is an entrepreneur or even that he is performing any entrepreneurial duties. People involved in the day-to-day management of a company—the office manager, the accountant, and perhaps even the president himself—are only common (or perhaps uncommon) labor. The jobs they perform can be filled from labor markets concerned with their particular skills. Only when these managers exercise the functions of innovation, major changes in production plans, etc, do they become entrepreneurs. By the same token, the man operating a small store may be an entrepreneur, but chances are that he will also be the bookkeeper, the clerk, the office boy, etc.. His earnings will come from performance of *all* these activities. If you add up the wages he could earn outside his own business in doing these various jobs and you find that there is something left over (other than earnings from his capital goods, such as the store or his inventory), these extra earnings come from his entrepreneurial efforts.

Now that we've talked about all the factors of production, we are faced with the question of *how* to produce various goods. How is it decided whether to use a lot of capital and little labor in producing an automobile or whether to have one large shop in which many men using only hand tools painstakingly piece cars together? Several things will influence this decision. First of all, the relative scarcity of the several factors is obviously going to have quite an impact on the choice. If there is a lot of idle capital equipment around which can be used to produce cars, and at the same time skilled workers are very hard to find, one would *try* to use more capital and less labor than might otherwise be the case. Certainly, in a planned economy, a planner would try to use available resources as fully as possible. But without a planner, the freely operating market for factors of production can also force the same decision. Obviously, the available technology—the possible ways of producing something from a technical viewpoint—will limit the choices available to either a planned or market solution. In any event, given the available technology, either the market or the economic planner will attempt to produce the desired output by using the combination of factors that will be cheapest. Here we are, back at the old business of cost again. Let's take a look now at the costs involved in producing something—costs of production.

There are only two possible places that resources received from the production of a good (probably received through the medium of money) can go. These resources can be paid out to the several factors of production that made the good or they can be *profit*. Before we discuss profit, let's take a look at payment of factors of production.

Why pay any factor of production anything? The answer is twofold. First, a factor of production must produce something of value—something valued by someone sufficiently to make them willing to *pay* for it. This payment from the demander of the good makes it *possible* to pay the factor. However, only if the factor is *scarce* will it be necessary to pay for it. An example might help. Most of you realize that it is absolutely essential that your automobile have air in order to run. Without air (or more properly, the oxygen in the air), the engine won't do a thing. Therefore, if you consider the *productivity* of the air around you in providing automobile transportation, the air is immensely *productive*. But generally, air of sufficient quantity to run your car is readily available. It is *not* scarce in that you can get all you want without giving up anything else. As a result, you don't have to pay for this very productive factor of production. On the other hand, something can be scarce without being productive, and again, it will be paid nothing as a factor of production. In between the various moonshots, air on the moon is very scarce. We could put some up there, at considerable cost. But unless man or some experiment requiring air was also there, air on the moon would not be productive. Therefore, people would not be willing to pay anything for it. Payments to factors, then, are made because they are *productive* and economically *scarce*.

In a market system, the maximum paid to factors will be the value of what they produce. If there are elements in the market that prevent free competition in the buying and selling of either the *product* or the factors themselves, then the factors could receive *less* than the value of what they produce. This point is vitally important and should be remembered. In a market system, if a factor doesn't *produce* the value, it can't be *paid* the value. This fact is often ignored by those who attack such problems as poverty. If you expect the market to reward labor, for example, that labor must be producing something of value to the community which makes up the market. If the labor is not producing this value, some other methods will have to be worked out if the factor is to have any income.

We said that resources received from the sale of a good could also go into something called profit. Again, this word must be used carefully because it means different things to different people. When we use "profit," it refers to something that is left over after *all* factors of production have been paid the value of their product. This means that not only labor has been paid, but also the holders of capital goods, owners of natural resources, and even our old friend the entrepreneur. All of these factors contributed to the production of the good and therefore can expect to be paid for their efforts. Anything left over after these payments is *profit*, as defined by the economist. What it really represents is a payment *over and above* the minimum payment required to get the factor to produce. If one were to remove this type of profit from the factor, the factor would continue to work in the given employment. Another way of putting it is that the profit is the amount of payment over and above the factor's next-best employment opportunity. It is payment over and above *opportunity cost*. Sometimes economists call this payment *economic profit, excess profit*, or sometimes simply *economic rent*.

Since businessmen act pretty much like everyone else, they try to get as much *profit* as possible. They try to produce things which will yield a profit, and they stop producing things which yield losses. But if there are competitive markets around, and other people discover that some enterprise is making a lot more profit than most other enterprises, more businesses will tend to start producing this highly profitable item. As production goes up, the producers and sellers compete with each other in selling the increased output. This, in turn, drives the *price* of the good down, which reduces the level of profit. If the profit gets too small or becomes a loss, some businesses will cease producing the good. The decreased quantity on the market will be bid for by prospective buyers, tending to raise the price and increase levels of profit. Thus, the market, through the process of bidding prices up and down, causes profits to increase or decrease. This changing level of profits is the signal which the businessman uses to keep his production closely tied to the wishes of the buying public. He doesn't do this because he's a nice guy. He does it because the impersonal market forces him to do so. Therefore, if the competitive markets are operating freely, profits will be eliminated—at least in the long run. Labor will make a return on its efforts. Capital will receive a return based on its contribution. The entrepreneur will receive a return on his abilities. (Notice, a bookkeeper would probably call this return "profit." We don't. Profit exists only over and above this return to the entrepreneur.) If all profits or hopes of receiving profits were to be eliminated, the incentive for producers to either be efficient or to pay attention to their buying public would also be eliminated.

Notice one more thing. If *competition* were to be eliminated, then a businessman making a large profit could continue to enjoy that situation. No one else could enter the field to increase production, thus cutting prices and profits. Competition is essential if the market system is to serve the efficient production of goods and services. Anything that restrains competition tends to make it possible to produce the wrong quantities of the wrong product to be sold at the wrong price. I'm using "wrong" in a very special sense. In this case, wrong refers to the fact that inefficiency exists. It would be possible to get *more* satisfactions for the community with the same resources. How does this competitive system make for the efficient distribution of factors of production? Since factors are being paid from the sales of the product, profitable production means jobs for the factors. Unprofitable production means reduced jobs in that field and/or lower wages. Again, given the existence of alternatives, low wages or lack of employment opportunities tend to force factors into the production of other items where their opportunity is now relatively greater. This is quite obvious and reflects the way that you yourself would probably act.

There are a couple of other characteristics associated with costs of production that should be mentioned briefly. It would be convenient if all our actions in life were individually very small and could be retracted if they turned out to be less than perfect. Unfortunately, this is not the case. It's very difficult to buy 1/1000 of an automobile. True, you could buy a car with 999 other people and each of you could have a 1/1000 claim on the services from that automobile. Alternatively, you might rent an automobile for 1/1000 of its useful life. But generally, if you buy a car, you buy a whole car.

Now comes an interesting question. Having bought the car and paid the purchase price, what kinds of costs make you decide whether or not you're actually going to drive it? Clearly, every mile you drive will require gasoline—the more miles, the more gasoline; the less miles, the less gasoline. The same thing applies to the oil you use. It is also true of the wear on your tires, the expected repairs to your engine, and even the wear on your seat covers. If you're wondering whether or not to drive more miles with your car, the *additional expenses* these extra miles will cost influence the decision to drive or not drive. These are the costs that vary with use—variable costs. But how about the cost of the car itself? Will the price you paid for the car influence your decision to drive or not to drive *once the purchase is made*? The answer is no, or at least not much. Cars generally *depreciate*, that is, become less valuable, based on their *age* rather than the number of miles they have been driven. Sure, if you maintain a car and drive 200,000 miles in five years, it will probably be worth a little less than a car maintained and driven only 40,000 miles in the same period—a little less, but not much. Once you have purchased an automobile or anything else, the cost of *owning* it is *fixed*. There is nothing you can do to increase or decrease this cost until you trade the car in or buy a new one. The point of this whole discussion is that in making a decision to use or not use, to produce more or less, to do this thing or that, the only costs influencing that decision are variable costs. It is the *additional* cost of some action that must enter the decision-making rather than the *total* cost of the action.

Going back to the business of optimizing satisfactions, a businessman is also going to optimize his (or the company's) satisfactions by maximizing profits—making profits just as large as possible. Of course, this maximizing operation may take place over a long period so that, for instance, the business might be losing money right now because of substantial development costs. But this "loss" in the present might produce large profits in some future time period. Therefore, profit maximization in the long run might call for profit losses in the short run. Well then, does the businessman always minimize costs? Just as with the individual behavior discussed earlier, this is ridiculous. True, for any given *output* or any given level of *total revenue received*, he will try to produce that level as cheaply as possible. But basically, the businessman is interested in maximizing the *difference* between total receipts and total expenditures. In fact, he will choose that level of production which will maximize the difference between total receipts and total costs—the level of production at which *profits* are the greatest. He will *increase* production just as long as the receipts from the increased production are slightly larger than the expenses incurred by the increased production. If this is the case, profits will be increased. On the other hand, if increased production means that expenses go up more than the receipts, profits will *decrease*, and the businessman will attempt to reduce output. Figure 5.1 illustrates this idea using the same sort of set diagrams that were used in the satisfaction argument. It merely illustrates the same old point. It's not just the greatest possible income the enterprise is interested in, nor is it just the lowest possible cost. The name of the game is to make the difference between the two as large as possible (in the revenue *over* cost direction).

One more item must be covered in this discussion of costs. You've probably heard a great

Figure 5.1
Profit Maximization

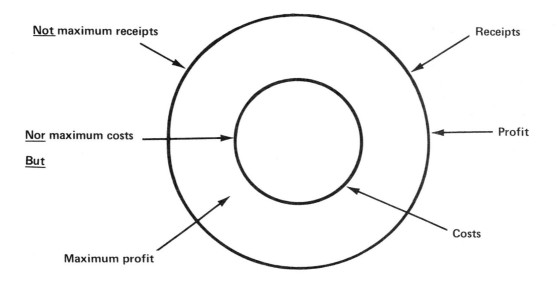

deal about the business of "economies of scale." The general idea that is all too generally accepted is that the larger the operation, the more efficient it is; therefore, big businesses are necessary in order to have reasonably priced products. What this argument implies is that as a business increases in size and producing capacity, the cost of producing one more unit is *less* than the cost of producing the unit just before it. The cost of producing the 10,000,000th automobile was $2,000 but the cost of producing the 10,000,001st automobile is only $1,900. As long as this pattern of costs exists, the bigger the plant, the cheaper the production; so let's make automobile plants as large as possible. In fact, let's have only *one* automobile plant to produce *all* the cars in the world. Well, that's quite an idea, but there are a few problems.

If this happens, competition has had it. We now have something called a *monopoly*—a single seller of the product. This means that the producer no longer has to worry about competitors stealing his customers if he doesn't keep his price as low as possible. He also doesn't have to worry as much about keeping the most efficient method of production in his plant. He now can control the total production of automobiles in the world, which gives him another advantage unavailable to a producer in a competitive situation. Now he can adjust output to lower levels *which will raise the price people are willing to pay*. He won't sell as many units as the competitive industry would have, but again, our monopolist isn't interested in maximizing *production* either. Just like his competitive counterpart, he is interested in maximizing *profit*, and if raising the price by cutting production will *add* to profit, he'll do it. However, don't get the idea (which many people have) that a monopoly can charge any price it wants to. The higher the price charged, the fewer will be the units sold. The producer is still *constrained* by what buyers are willing and able to pay. However, he can deal with just those people who want the product the most and are most able to pay high prices. Being a monopolist gives the added advantage of having the *choice* of *output* which will result in the *particular price per unit* which in turn will yield the *maximum profit*.

In actual fact, "economies of scale" are probably a much overrated idea. Most companies do not have decreasing costs beyond certain points. In fact, costs generally start to rise as bigness takes over. Whether in a government or a private bureaucracy, size begins to breed so-called administrative costs that can make any enterprise top-heavy. As a result, many of the arguments for increasing the size of any operation—private or public—really rest on a desire for increased control or power. Such control or power *can* be the death of an efficient market system.

Questions and Problems for Chapter 5

1.   Take everything out of your pockets, billfold, or purse. Consider the services yielded by each of the items in front of you. If you're like most people, probably many of the things there don't yield any services at all and you are carrying them just because you forgot to throw them out. On the other hand, consider how your life would be different without some of the items.

2.   Make a list of all the tools that you use in your school activities. Remember, any good which assists the educational process is considered a tool.

3. Many of you undoubtedly have part-time jobs. Make a list of the job alternatives you have now and the wages each would pay. Are you working in the job with the highest hourly wage? Why or why not?

4. Many of you have been brought up in families in which parents made most of the choice decisions for their young children. What would be the difference between this ruling body and a ruling body of planners in a controlled economy? Would you expect more or fewer problems of decision enforcement in the family group or the economy-wide group? Why?

5. Why are wages to labor so low in a country like India? Suggest several things that might be done to raise those wages.

6. In some countries where labor is very cheap, goods are still produced using a great deal of capital and comparatively little labor. How can this situation be explained?

7.   "All that needs to be done to solve the problem of poverty is to tax the rich and give it to the poor." Comment on this proposition. Would anyone besides the "rich" pay for this solution?

8.   How much do you save at this time? Do you receive interest on your savings? If someone offered to pay you two dollars next week for every dollar you loaned them today, what would you do? Would you work more today? Would you spend more today?

9. Going back to your part-time job, if your wage rate was doubled, would this make you better off or worse off? How might it make you worse off?

10. If, all of a sudden, you were the only person around who could perform the job you are being paid for, what would you do? What would your employer do? What would the customers for your employer's product do?

Now we have all these goods *produced*, and we've assumed that somehow the production is tied to the desires and abilities of the community. There's another step that must be undertaken, at least in complex industrial economies. In general, it is more efficient to concentrate production of goods into specialized locations. These locations may be called factories, plants, farms, or some other title. The main thing, however, is that concentrating production means that the product is probably separated somewhat from many of the persons that want to buy and use the good. This *distribution* problem deserves a little consideration because many aspects of it affect you all the time—sometimes quite significantly.

The phrase "free market" has been used to describe the uninhibited interaction of buyers and sellers. It's fine to talk about a free market in this sense, but in another sense, the market *operation* is anything *but* free. Transferring useful property rights from one individual or entity to another individual or entity requires the use of resources. It will *cost* something to make the transfer. In this chapter, for convenience, we will break down these transfer costs into *transactions costs, transportation costs,* and *handling costs.* This breakdown is quite arbitrary and doesn't have any particular significance except convenience.

Looking first at transactions costs, we must further separate these into more specific categories. Every transaction involves buyers and sellers gaining or having a certain amount of *information.* Often, this information costs somebody something to obtain. In other words, transactions usually involve some *informational costs.* It may be no more than a $2.00 advertisement in the classified section of the newspaper. On the other hand, it may be a $100,000 television commercial. In either case, however, something is expended; someone is going to pay for the resources used. Earlier, we mentioned the housewife who spent her entire day shopping in different food stores. This is a good example of an informational cost in the lives of most consumers. In the case of the housewife, it might well turn out that her expenses of obtaining market information exceed any possible saving in food costs. In fact, it is this that makes it possible for several stores in the same area to sell similar items at somewhat different prices. U.S. Choice grade rib steak may be selling at Friendly Joe's for $.98 per pound and at the same time, Slim Jim's is selling the same quality item for $.94 per pound. If a housewife is interested in buying four pounds for tonight's dinner, she could save $.16 if she knows that Slim Jim's has the lower price. However, if getting this information means she has to make a special trip to Slim Jim's the cost of that trip in both her time and travel expenses might easily outweigh any potential saving. In many cities, newspaper advertising is widely used for passing on information about food prices. It is comparatively cheap, and the written prices make it easy for customers to compare alternative prices on a wide variety of grocery items. I'm sure you've already realized from this brief presentation that a *competitive* market system really depends heavily on the availability of accurate information on alternative prices. If allocation decisions are being made by a planning elite, then such information on price alternatives becomes unnecessary since there are no alternatives.

Every transfer of property rights in some good from seller to buyer involves a *contract* or agreement between the two parties. The contract may consist of nothing more than a handshake or might be a 100-page document that requires a battery of lawyers to write or interpret. Again, more often than not, forming these agreements involves expenditure of resources—resources in the form of *contractual costs*. Even the simple act of checking out at the local supermarket is a contractual cost. Explicitly, the girl operating the cash register must be paid as must the capital investment in the cash register itself. From your standpoint, the time you spend in the line presumably has an alternative use. This means that again you suffer an opportunity cost in waiting for the "contract" to be made at the checkout desk. Some transactions in which you are liable to become involved contain very substantial contractual costs. Buying a home, for instance, will include paying *closing costs*. These include drawing up the new deed by a lawyer, checking out the title to the property to make sure the seller actually owns the real estate, etc. You may have also paid a substantial information cost in the form of a commission to a real estate agent. You might argue that this cost is actually paid by the seller. After all, you paid the real estate broker, say, $35,000 for the house. The broker kept his cut of let's say 7 percent or $2,450 and paid the balance of $32,550 to the previous owner. Your facts may be right, but don't you ever believe that you, the buyer, are not paying at least some of this fee. Remember, if it had been possible for you and the owner to find each other without the services of the broker, there would have been $2,450 which could either have been "saved" by you or "gained" by the seller. In all probability, the selling price would have been somewhat lower, with each of you gaining from the reduced information cost. But don't think I'm recommending that you disregard real estate brokers. On the contrary, they *can* provide much cheaper market information than either you or the seller could do on your own.

Returning for a moment to the contractual cost idea, there is an important point to be made in this category. The more complex the "deal" is, the more expensive will be the contractual costs. Simple, clean transfers of ownership generally involve fairly small contracting costs. If you're buying a home, and there is nothing special about the deal, the chances are that your lawyer or agent will simply use a standard form for such transactions in your state, expenses of closing the deal will be minimal. On the other hand, if there are all sorts of qualifications involved in the sale, up go the contractual costs. If the seller decides that he wants first crack at the property should *you* decide to resell (a right of first refusal), this will involve a more complicated and expensive contract. Also, if property rights are poorly defined in the laws of the area, a "safe" contract may require substantial costs of research and checking to see just what is involved. For example, in many areas water rights are poorly defined. If there is a stream running through your property, your rights to that stream are not always as simple as you might think. Since the stream originates on someone else's land, there are special joint issues between you and that property owner. Again, since the stream passes on to another person's land, you will have potential problems dealing with your mutual rights in the stream and its waters. In some states, these water rights are carefully spelled out and a long history of legal precedence has been established. In other states or municipalities, this is not the case. Exchanges of rights in these areas then become both expensive and unsure—there is a risk in the security of your rights.

There is a final category of transactions cost that is usually overlooked because it has nothing to do with the actual sale or purchase at the time the sale or purchase takes place. For a *right* to be a *right*, it must exist. For it to exist, either everyone must agree voluntarily and without exception to the existence of the right *or* the right must be enforced by someone. Men being what they are, there seems to be no escaping the necessity of *policing* whatever rights structure the community decides to adopt. This may be a structure based primarily on *private property rights*, or *community property rights*, or some combination of both. Whatever the case, once established, property rights must be enforced if they are to have any meaning at all. The enforcing will again require expenditure of resources, and we will have *policing costs*. Another point should be noted here. Complex property right structures may require interpretation, and this interpretation may involve spending resources. Honest differences of opinions often need to be settled by a third party. Here again, this will cost.

Let's see what some of the ramifications of "Law and Order" are in economic terms. First of all, if everyone *did* agree to respect property rights (whatever the agreed-upon structure was), then there would be no need for policing, and hence no policing costs. A community which is very "moral" in that it respects and abides by the existing rules of the game, whatever they are, requires very little policing. Even a dynamic society which changes the rules, but changes them according to agreed-upon guidelines still has little problem in the policing cost department.

What happens, however, when this morality breaks down—when people begin to break the rules of property? If you're one of the "breakers," you will probably say the society starts to oppress you. If you're one against whom the infringements are taking place, you'll start screaming for better protection. Regardless of your position, policing costs are going to rise. Lack of morality, whatever that morality is, will cost the community increases in policing expenditures. Many revolutionaries, being aware of this, use the tactic of attempting to break up a society's property system. This is true for all kinds of revolutionaries, be they Marxist or Minutemen.

To sum up, there are three types of costs involved in exchanging property rights. Information on both the buyer's and seller's part is required. Exchange will require some kind of contractual agreement between buyer and seller. Finally, the rights exchanged must be enforced if the exchange is to have any real meaning. All of these phases of transactions—information, contractual, and policing—generally require the expenditure of resources. Because of this, transactions costs themselves must be examined as an important part of everyday economic life.

Transportation Costs—Man has been engaged in space programs ever since he got started on this earth—not the ones to the moon or Mars, but the ones of getting from Point A across some spatial distance to Point B. As mentioned at the beginning of this chapter, specialization of any sort usually means that the products man wants will be produced at some distance from the consumer. Not everyone will have an automobile factory literally in his backyard, nor a brewery in his front yard. The whole business of specialization to improve efficiency implies that areas also will become specialized. Bananas will be grown in tropical areas where the resources expended to grow bananas are less than those that would be required in northern Wisconsin. Bananas *could* be grown in northern Wisconsin, but think what you would need to pull it off. Greenhouses with fantastic heat requirements as well as high intensity lights would be required just for openers.

By the same token, complicated goods *could* be made by people producing bits and pieces in their homes. In the early days of the so-called Industrial Revolution, such "cottage industry" was fairly common. Increased levels of specialization, however, have made the factory the most efficient location for producing most of the industrial goods we use. But this specialization of location has mean that *transportation* has become an increasingly important part of the production/distribution/consumption system. Developing transportation makes it possible to take advantage of specialized characteristics of different locations. It also helps maintain the all-important competition within the markets. Decreasing transportation costs means that a given market may quite possibly be served by many more suppliers. Suppliers farther from the given market now find that their total costs have fallen due to decreased transportation costs. This allows them to compete with other suppliers closer to the market. A good example of this phenomenon occurred ten or fifteen years ago when large-volume air freight was just becoming available. Prior to this time, you might find a few fresh Mexican strawberries in border markets during the wintertime. They were generally of poor quality and had a reputation for causing problems that some people called "Montezuma's Revenge." Mass air freight development provided an economical way to ship fresh strawberries directly from Mexico City to the major metropolitan areas of New York and Chicago. This, in turn, provided an incentive for Mexican growers to improve both the quality of their product and their incomes as well. Some of our own southern states screamed like crazy at all this. They made extravagant claims about the inferior quality of the imported product and hinted broadly that it was unpatriotic to buy this fruit. Of course, their main problem was the increased competition that this new source provided. This in turn was the result of improved transportation—improved in the sense of decreased cost. More on this topic will be presented in Chapter 15.

Often, the various types of transportation seem to fall into the category of enterprises that *might* be most efficient in some kind of quasi-monopoly situation. As a result, governments at various levels get involved in the important management decisions of the companies such as pricing—setting up rate structures for moving people and commodities. Without commenting on the propriety of this government intervention, it should be noted that by setting different transportation rates, the governments have a very powerful tool which could not only affect the transportation companies and their profits, but also could affect the whole business of who can find it profitable to produce where. Very often transportation companies, or the regulating governmental agencies, will establish different rates for hauling different goods. This *differential pricing* means that one producer may be able to have his goods hauled for $.02 per pound per mile while a producer of another good may find that he has to pay $.04 per pound per mile. Some of the differences in rates may be the result of differing costs of handling, but often the differentials are merely a way of charging each group the most that the companies (or government regulating bodies) think the customers can pay. Again, this is not to say that such a price policy is good or bad. But it does show the importance of transportation pricing.

As with anything that increases specialization, transportation development means that we all become increasingly interdependent. To provide our wants, we tend to depend less on ourselves and more on the complex of others which specialization has created. Again, this isn't an issue of right and wrong, but rather an issue of economic efficiency. We can get more for less if we rely even more heavily on each other. But this interdependence is not without its cost. It means that any kind of economic isolation becomes very expensive. It means too that conflicts in any form can upset the whole system. *Peace* is absolutely essential for a smoothly functioning economic system based on specialization.

Our final category of distribution costs consists of the resources expended in handling goods in the process of getting them from producer to user. The first that will be considered at this stage is *storage and inventories*. The two ideas are so tied together that we'll consider it a single concept.

I remember a wonderful old house in which I was born. It was built sometime in the 1860's in a little village which really hadn't changed much—nor has it changed much today. In the basement of this home there was a room called a fruitcellar. While the rest of the basement had a concrete floor, this room had a dirt floor. Even when empty, the fruitcellar had a smell that has never been equaled anywhere. It truly was a smell of life, and earth, and food, and security, and even mild affluence. Each fall, the crates and baskets of fruits and vegetables started filling this great dank, cool cavern, and for the rest of the winter, *this* was where the apples and potatoes and carrots and onions and cabbage, and squash kept coming from. Buy this sort of thing in the grocery store? Buy four pounds of apples at a time? Ridiculous! Of course, by spring, even my wonderful room was unable to hold back the processes of life and death any longer. The old potatoes and onions began sprouting new life while the apples at the bottom of the baskets began to give out a wine-like aroma. Eating apples increasingly gave way to apple pie and applesauce as smooth hard flesh gave way to the rubbery wrinkles of old age.

Why has all this changed? What happened to the good old fruitcellar and quantity purchases of fine produce direct from the farmer? The answer to these questions is complex indeed, but the more important reasons can be viewed fairly simply. First of all, housewives have become very conscious of the *quality* of food—particularly from the standpoint of *appearance*. A bruised apple, a pale-colored apple, an apple with a wormhole in it—all these things are undesirable. Fruits and vegetables such as those stored for months in a fruitcellar would be summarily tossed out by most of today's homemakers. The cost of *space*, enclosed space, such as the fruitcellar, has also gone up in terms of what must be sacrificed to get it. Most homes today don't have space that their owners are willing to commit to inventories of foodstuffs. They prefer a "family room" instead. It is cheaper to let a storage specialist handle the storage function. Of course, this also means that the storage is probably better. Improved storage technology makes it possible to keep fresh produce much longer than a generation ago.

What about the friendly farmer from whom you could buy direct? Well, in some cases you still can. Roadside markets still exist in which a farm family sells the fruit of their collective or individual labors. But most often, the farmer also has bowed to the increase in specialization. The time it took him to sell you one bushel of apples could probably have been used to sell 1,000 bushels of apples to a wholesaler. True, he'll get less money *per bushel* from the wholesaler, but the wholesaler will not perform many of the sales and distribution functions formerly done by the farmer himself.

Finally, how about all this packaging nonsense that pollutes our environment and makes container manufacturers rich? This increased use of packaging is the natural outgrowth of all the other points we've just mentioned. Smaller available storage means sales in smaller units. Increased central storage again means smaller sales more often. Increased labor costs mean more emphasis on mechanized packaging instead of the local grocery clerk bagging up stuff. Sure it costs. However, Mrs. Housewife seems willing and able to pay the cost. If "she" really wanted to go back to the good old days, the market would be glad to oblige. The fact is that despite the protestations to the contrary, a large number of buyers actually prefer—and pay for—the new ways. Of course, the pollution aspect brings up the point of whether or not the buyers of packaged goods *are* paying all that they should. More on this in Chapter 8.

Gimmicks—Distribution in any country or system has its gimmicks. Even the much touted systems of the socialist countries have the equivalent of the Anacin ad. They may be peddling politics instead of pills, but the principle is the same. The most widely used gimmick is, of course, *advertising*. As you all know, advertising is supposed to provide potential buyers information which will assist them in making a rational choice between the product advertised and some alternative. It is supposed to provide the means for the buying public to learn about the latest innovations and improvements. It is supposed to provide information, *economic information*, and we have already seen how important this is to the efficient operation of a market economy. The question is whether advertising *does* perform these necessary functions or whether it merely brainwashes by constant repetition of misleading and superfluous nonsense. If the latter is the case, are expenditures on advertising a complete waste or do they have any economic impact?

Almost all advertising *does* perform some of the informational functions noted above. Most advertising also tends to overstate the case of the particular producer. Therefore, it is safe to say that the case for or against advertising in general can't be general. Without any advertising, our market system would be in bad shape due to the difficulty of obtaining information. Further, available research, though limited, tends to support the idea that real brainwashing through the media doesn't work too well *unless* the product performs reasonably well too. If this is the case, why do huge companies spend millions upon millions of dollars trying to sell people one form of aspirin versus another from of aspirin when all they're really selling is just aspirin?

Again, the answer is not simple but some of it can be presented here. These kinds of companies are not *monopolists*, but they are sellers in an industry where a few large companies dominate the market. Each of these companies *does compete* with the others, but the competition takes on the form of competing for the other guy's market through *advertising* rather than *price*. If they were in a truly competitive industry, this would be impossible since expenditures on this kind of advertising would be wasted. Each competitor could have all the sales he wished *at the market price*, and there would be no incentive to advertise other than for information. But our friendly aspirin peddlers are trying their best (and succeeding in a few cases) to convince the buying public that they are not peddling aspirin (which *is* a good pain killer), but rather selling God's gift for the hangover or the common cold or whatever. Each is trying to *differentiate* his product from the products of other producers. In doing so, he hopes to establish a monopoly position with at least *some* customers. How can you fight this kind of thing? Simple! First of all, support laws that require truth in advertising. This might help. Secondly, don't buy the bums' products. If there is a choice of the same stuff, buy the non-named product. Of course, be sure it *is* the same product. What are the impacts of "differentiation advertising"? Basically, resources are transferred from the buying public to the companies, and from the companies to the viewers of soap operas, listeners of classical music programs, watchers of the late-late show, etc. Maybe this is the way the community wants things organized. On the other hand, there might be more efficient ways to support radio, television, the theater, and the arts. Perhaps advertising should be rolled back to its economic function of providing useful market information.

A final word on gimmicks in general. Like everything else, gimmicks cost. Often, however, they are made to seem as though they were free. Again, and again, and again, "There ain't no such thing as a free lunch!" Trading stamps are not free. The cost of the merchandise they can "purchase" is hidden in the products you're buying. Doesn't it make more sense for people to have *money* with which they can buy anything they want, rather than having stamps with which they can get some gadget they didn't *buy* before? If you're getting stamps and cheaper prices too, fine. But those "cheaper prices" *could be* cheaper still without the stamps. How about "easy payments"? We'll be spending quite a bit of time on this on in Chapter 10, so now we'll just say that easy payments may make your budgeting simpler, but you're going to pay a higher price, and don't forget it! Finally, how about stores that sell something at less than they pay for it just to get you to come in and buy something else too? To handle this one, just go in and buy the "loss-leader" item, but *nothing else*. You'll not only drive the seller nuts, but out of business as well. Be careful though. The time you waste is your own!

Questions and Problems for Chapter 6

1. List all the purchases you have made in the last week. Were there any transactions costs involved in these purchases? List them according to whether they were informational, contractual, or policing.

2. What transactions costs might have been included in the price of the product initially but were paid for by the producer or seller? In terms of your buying the product, would it have made any difference if you had paid the transactions cost yourself rather than the seller paying it?

3. Go to the drugstore where you can best trust the pharmacist and list the prices for different brands of aspirin (5 grain tablets). Ask the pharmacist what the differences between the different brands are. Do the same thing for three or four other drug products whose contents the pharmacist can identify precisely.

4. Right now most of our commercial television is financed by advertising of commercial products. Who really pays the bill for the television programs? Discuss among yourselves some alternatives for financing entertainment television.

5. For those of you that either live at home or are doing your own housekeeping, check carefully for one week the price advertisements for major foodstores, and shop to buy the cheapest. Keep track of the savings you accomplish over shopping your usual way. Also keep track of your extra expenses such as transportation, your own time, etc.

6. Take the price or market value of the residence in which you live. Calculate the total cubic feet of usable space in the residence, and then find the value per cubic foot. Now you can see one of the many reasons why small unit purchases are popular today.

7. Many professional and semi-professional groups have trade or business associations through which fees for services (usually a minimum fee) are agreed upon. This means that "cheap operators" are not allowed to undercut the established rates. What are some of the pros and cons of this arrangement for the professionals? For their customers?

8.   If the government decided to provide all the transportation services anyone wanted from any place in the U.S. to any other place in the U.S. without charge to the users, what kinds of effects would you expect? Who would benefit and who would pay? Would you expect areas to specialize in producing goods for which they were most adapted?

9.   Take a trip down to your local supermarket and see if you can get the manager to spend half an hour giving you the pros and cons of pre-packaging operations. The chances are that he can even give you numbers on the costs involved in this operation and the savings in waste.

10.   List ways other than price in which companies can compete with each other. Can you think of some reasons why this non-price competition might weaken the price system?

General Determinants of Demand—In Chapter 1, we talked about people's desires or wants, and in the last couple chapters we have talked briefly about something called *demand*. Demand is merely the combination of someone's willingness or desire to get something *plus his ability to get something*. The old saying, "Talk's cheap, but it takes money to buy good whiskey," illustrates this point. For the economist, this ability to purchase distinguishes all the limitless wants in the world from the possible means of satisfying those wants. Again, you may think that this analysis implies the capitalist system of free markets, etc. It *can* imply that, but it *doesn't have to*. The planned societies have the same problem of deciding how to allocate the scarce items available, so they too must combine some type of ability to pay with people's desires for goods. However, much of what follows deals specifically with the market system and the market mechanism—not necessarily the "perfect" market of total competition—but market operations nonetheless.

What are the basic determinants of a person's willingness and ability to purchase some good? One of these is how badly he wants the services that can be gained from using the good. Fortunately, the market provides a visible mechanism for these wants to be reflected—reflected in comparative terms with others who also want the particular good. The market, in effect, asks each potential buyer, "What are you prepared to give up in order to get this item?" If money is being used in the system, the answer to the question can be expressed in money terms. "I will give up five dollars for one unit of the good." The five dollars, of course, is nothing more than a measure of *other* potential purchases that are being sacrificed (not made) to purchase the good in question. One could just as easily say, "I will give up one economics textbook to get the desired good." In this case the price of the good is one textbook rather than five dollars. This is still just as legitimate a price as the dollar figure. *Price* is that which must be given up to get one unit of something else. It could be expressed in books or wheat or jellybeans just as well—not as conveniently, but just as possibly. The higher the price of anything, the more that must be given up to get it. Simple as that! Well, then, it clearly follows that the more one has to give up to get something else, the more he must want that something else. The *price of the product* will be an important determinant of the quantity that will be demanded of that product. Notice also, if one person is willing and able to pay more for a good than you are, he will compete with you for the purchase. In doing so, the price will be "bid up." If it gets too high, you'll drop out of the bidding process (the market) and the guy that wanted it the most will get it. Of course, he may be able to get it just because he has more resources to give up than you do. His income (what he takes in per week, month, or year) or his accumulated wealth (the stock of resources he can control) may make his ability to buy greater than yours. This brings us to the next important determinant of demand—the incomes of the potential buyers.

If someone asked you for a quick answer to the question, "How do the incomes of buyers affect the quantity of a good they will demand?" your answer would probably be that the higher the incomes of demanders, the greater would be their demand for a good. You would be only partly right with this answer. If you were talking about the demand for Rolls-Royce automobiles or prime-cut sirloin steak, your response would be just right. For these types of goods (the economists call them "normal" or "superior" goods), as incomes go up, so does the quantity demanded by potential buyers.

Before we go any further, there is a way of viewing economic problems that needs a bit of explaining. Some of you are probably already asking what will happen if *two* things happen at the same time. For example, what would happen if the *price* of a normal good went up, and, at the same time, the incomes of the potential buyers went up? The answer is that you can't tell unless you have actual facts and figures from the market concerned. The increased price of the good tends to *decrease* the quantity demanded. The rising incomes of demanders tend to increase the quantity demanded of the good. Therefore, the two forces tend to offset each other, and without actual facts and numbers from that specific market, it's as far as we can go.

To analyze economic problems, and many problems in other disciplines as well, each force is viewed separately. (I know, in the real world, they *aren't* separate, but even in the real world it *is* possible to use techniques that effectively separate complex events into their component parts.) Conceptually, we hold all things constant except two variables, and then we see how those two variables interact with each other. For example, if we wish to see how the price of a good is related to the quantity demanded of that good, we try to hold all other factors constant that might also affect the quantity demanded—all factors except the price of the good itself. If we then wish to see how the incomes of demanders affect the quantity demanded, we again hold everything else constant (now including the price of the good) and look just at the relationship of incomes to quantity demanded. Modern statistical techniques make this dream world possible. Often one can obtain an "everything else being equal" world in which the effects of different variables can be determined or estimated by themselves.

Returning to our discussion of incomes, we find another category of goods whose demand will be adversely affected by increased incomes. What do you think will happen to the quantity of navy beans demanded when incomes rise in this country? I can tell you. Everything else being equal (including the price of the beans), the quantity demanded will *fall* as incomes *rise*. We call goods like these *inferior goods*—the higher the incomes of demanders, the lower the quantity demanded. Actually, there are many goods like these. Grains used for human food generally follow this pattern. Why? Because as incomes increase, people tend to eat more meat products and more fresh vegetables and fruit. The old cornmeal and wheat flour products fall out of favor due to people's ability to get higher-priced products with their increased incomes and buying power.

Another set of variables that will influence the quantity demanded of any particular good is the price structure of so-called *related goods*—goods that are either *substitutes for* or *complements to* the good concerned. Let's look at some examples. General Motors Corporation has an automobile called a Vega. They hope that this car is a substitute for (among others) Volkswagen. It is clearly *not* the same product as a VW, but many of the services derivable from the Vega can also be derived from the VW, and vice versa. How do you suppose the *price* of one of these cars would affect the *quantity demanded* of the other? If there is any substitutability *at all*, a decrease in the price of Vega will decrease the *demand* for VW's. Similarly, if the price of VW's falls, the *quantity demanded* of Vegas will fall. If two goods can be at least partially usable in the same function, then a fall in the price of one will cause people to substitute the now-cheaper alternative at the expense of the relatively more expensive alternative.

The other category of related goods is *complements*. When you buy a car you probably also buy four of five rubber tires. Now, you could drive the car without the tires, but the city would be a bit unhappy with the way you tear up their streets. You'd be a bit uncomfortable with the bumpy ride, too. The use of automobiles and automobile tires generally goes together. They are *complementary goods*. If the *price* of automobiles goes up, then chances are that people will buy fewer cars *and fewer tires*. In other words, if the *price* of automobiles goes up, the *demand* for tires goes down. There's nothing complicated about this notion at all. If two or more goods are generally used together, then the cost of using the total package is important. If the price of any good in the package goes up, then the cost of the total package goes up. Therefore, the demand for all the other goods in the package will decrease. Notice, the relationship between price and demand for complements is just the opposite of the relationship between price and demand for substitutes. For complements, price and demand are inversely related; for substitutes, price and demand are directly related.

The next item in the list of general determinants of demand is people's *tastes*. We're not going to dwell on or define this item too carefully at this level. We'll simply say that all of the subjective things that go into likes and dislikes, such as those reflected in styles, fads, or "in" things, are summed up in the variable, tastes. As people's taste for some good increases, obviously the quantity that will be demanded will also increase. As styles or fads change and people's taste for the good decreases, so will their willingness to purchase the good at any given price. You'll notice that clothes of last year's cut and style are often discounted in sales. The discounting reflects the fact that potential buyers are no longer willing to pay the same price for the same quantity of the good. Last year's style is gone and, with it, the demand for items reflecting that style.

Finally, the now well-developed idea of marketing costs—transactions costs—can also influence the quantity of any good that may be demanded. If it is necessary that a potential buyer spend a lot of time, energy, and perhaps money to get information about the things he might buy, his demand for those things will be decreased. Similarly, if closing the deal is going to be expensive, these high contract costs will also tend to reduce his demand. Lastly, if many resources are going to be required to enforce the property rights he buys, our demander will again reduce the quantity he is willing to purchase at any given price. Transactions costs for demanders can also be viewed as complements to the good itself. In other words, buying a house also means paying for the information services of a real estate broker, the contracting services of a lawyer, and municipal taxes, part of which will pay for the cop on the beat who protects your purchase. In one sense, at least, the transactions costs and the good itself are complements—the purchase of one probably implies the purchase of the other.

Market Operations—We haven't really mentioned it explicitly up to this point, but what you have covered in the last few chapters includes a couple of old ideas that economists have been kicking around for a good many years. Most of you have probably heard the perennial question, "What determines the *price* of something?" What? Supply and demand, of course. We've just finished talking about demand and, in discussing the production of things, we covered supply in a very elementary way. Now let's put the two ideas together and see how they interact. In Figure 7.1, we have shown the situation that might exist in which people's willingness and ability to buy something exceeded the willingness and ability of the community's suppliers to produce it. There are several ways that this imbalance or *disequilibrium* could be corrected. One of these ways is for the price of the good to be increased. Doing so would result in two different reactions. For most goods, increasing the price would mean that an incentive would appear for people to produce *more*. Why? Because producing this good at a higher price would likely result in higher *profits* than producing something else with similar inputs. Resources would be attracted into this industry *and out of other industries*. Quantity supplied would tend to increase as in Figure 7.2. At the same time, a higher price for the product would mean that potential buyers would have to give up more for the good than they did before. More would have to be sacrificed per unit of the product. This will tend to lower the quantity demanded, shrinking it as in Figure 7.2. If the price is increased just the right amount, it will exactly equate people's willingness and ability to purchase with other people's

Figure 7.1
The Market

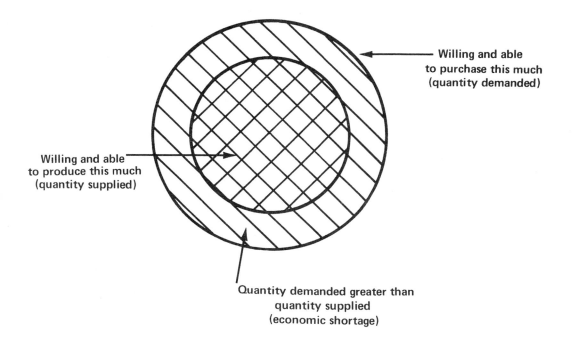

Willing and able
to purchase this much
(quantity demanded)

Willing and able
to produce this much
(quantity supplied)

Quantity demanded greater than
quantity supplied
(economic shortage)

Figure 7.2
The Market with Price Increase

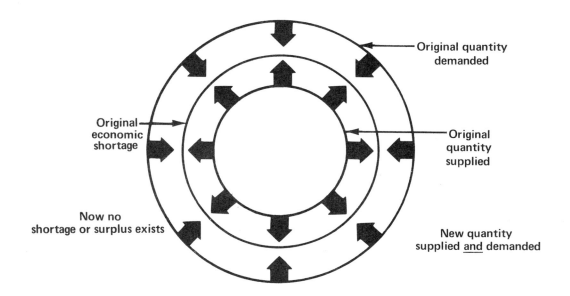

Original quantity
demanded

Original
economic
shortage

Original
quantity
supplied

Now no
shortage or surplus exists

New quantity
supplied and demanded

willingness and ability to sell. Equilibrium will be established. Quantity supplied will exactly equal quantity demanded.

Notice, I've suggested that the price was raised by some force or other from the "too low" level that resulted in a shortage, to a "just right" level which brought about equilibrium. Does this action have to come from some authority, or will it happen by itself? The answer is that, given free operation of a market, the price movement will be automatic. Think about it for a moment. In the case of our shortage price, demanders of the good are going to start bidding among themselves for the limited quantity available. There are other things they might do instead of bidding up the price, such as drawing straws or flipping a coin. They might also decide to just plain wait in line so that the first people in the line would get the good while those at the end would go without. But if people are allowed to use a free market mechanism to decide who gets the scarce goods, the resulting bidding process will result in a higher price. Price will rise without any direction from anyone. Again, the increased price will tend to reduce the quantity demanded by people and also raise the quantity people are willing and able to supply. Both reactions to the increased price move in the right direction for removing the original shortage.

As you might suspect, there is another side of this same coin. Assume that, for some reason, a price exists in a market *above* the free equilibrium level. Such a situation is illustrated in Figure 7.3a. With too high a price, the quantity people are willing and able to supply exceeds the quantity other people are willing and able to purchase. The result is an economic *surplus*. More of this particular good is around than *the market* can get rid of. What pressures will exist in this case? Now, since suppliers are unable to get rid of their stocks at the high price, there will be a tendency to cut prices in order to move the good. These cut-rate prices will generally encourage *more people* to buy *more*. Quantity demanded will go up. At the same time, the lower price will discourage continuation of the same level of production. Suppliers will tend to reduce the quantity supplied. Both of these reactions tend to correct the original surplus condition until the price is low enough to bring quantities supplied and demanded into equilibrium. This happy state is shown in Figure 7.3b. Lowering the market price will eliminate the surplus condition. This lower price will *just happen* if a free market is allowed to develop and operate.

If this business of the price of the good is so important in allocating economic goods, then just *how much* the quantities demanded or supplied actually change with given changes in price is certainly an important question. If you are sick and the doctor says you must have a shot of penicillin if you are to recover, probably the *second* thing you'll ask is how much it costs. The *first* thing you'll ask is how soon you can get it. In this instance, the importance of price or even price changes in influencing the quantity people are going to demand is probably quite low. You'd still buy the shot if it cost $.50 or $20.00. You'd buy the amount the doctor ordered, no more, no less; and the price of the shot wouldn't matter much.

Things that people view as necessities tend to display this lack of responsiveness to price

Figure 7.3
The Market with Lower Price

a.

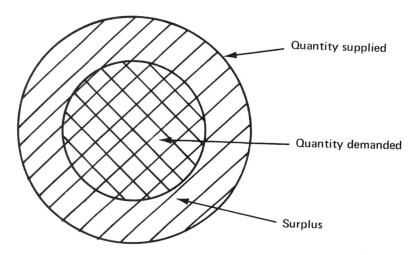

Quantity supplied

Quantity demanded

Surplus

b.

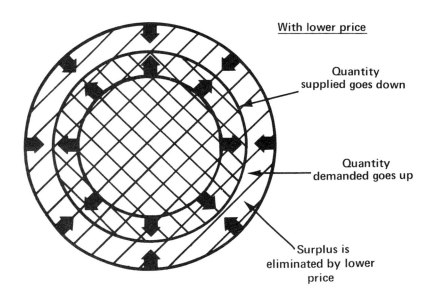

With lower price

Quantity supplied goes down

Quantity demanded goes up

Surplus is eliminated by lower price

changes. These goods are said to have *inelastic* demands. Similarly, things which represent a very small purchase within your budget tend to have inelastic demands. The classic example often used is table salt. It's very unlikely that the quantity of table salt you buy depends very much on the price of the salt. If a twelve-cent box went to twenty-five cents, your purchases (and most other people's) wouldn't change much. If for some reason the price went to a hundred dollars per box, this would no longer be the case. A doubling of the price when the price is that large would undoubtedly have a significant influence on the quantity of the good demanded. It's no longer a purchase of little consequence to your pocketbook. Now it approaches a major expenditure. The mirror image of these points also tends to be true. Goods that represent "luxury" purchases to the buyer will generally be comparatively responsive in terms of price changes and corresponding changes in quantities demanded. Also, if some good has a lot of substitutes, the quantity demanded will probably vary tremendously with comparatively small changes in price. People will switch (into or out of) the substitute items should much of a price change take place in the market for the given good. If few or no substitutes are available, this option isn't open to the purchaser, and his demand for the given good will be less elastic. Notice, our whole discussion thus far has assumed that *price and only price* is the thing that brings about equilibrium. A few paragraphs from now you'll see that other things affecting quantity demanded can also bring about a form of equilibrium, but generally not in an automatic way.

For example, assume we're looking at the market of prime beef sirloin. Again, assume that the price of this product (a normal good) is too high for some reason and we have a surplus of sirloin around. If the price is not lowered, is there any other way the quantity demanded could be increased or the quantity supplied decreased? Of course. On the demand side, we could give all the potential demanders of sirloin an *income subsidy*. We will increase their buying power. This subsidy has the effect of raising incomes, which in turn raises the quantity demanded of sirloin. Increasing the demand moves in the direction of removing the surplus and attaining equilibrium. Similarly, you might *tax* the suppliers of sirloin, thus raising their costs and decreasing the quantity they would be willing and able to produce at any given price. This also will tend to reduce the surplus by cutting quantity supplied. The first action (income subsidy) will raise the quantity actually marketed while the second action (taxing the suppliers) will lower the quantity marketed.

Another type of action that could help bring about equilibrium would be an attempt to change people's tastes for sirloin. The meat industry might try mounting a huge advertising campaign designed to get people to eat more meat and less bread and potatoes. This action would increase the quantity demanded at any given price and reduce the original surplus condition. Of course, if you were a wheat or potato grower, you might be a bit upset by this attempt to steal your customers. In fact, you might get so upset that you decide a little counter-advertising is in order. The more your competitor spends to get your customers, the more you spend to get them back. The advertising companies make out very well in this fight, but the companies and their customers pay for it in higher prices and/or reduced quantities of *both* products on the market.

Take another example of trying to influence a market system by changing things other than just the price of the good. In the area of illegal and addictive drugs, this is precisely what some communities are attempting today. If one is a heroin user, and particularly if the pusher supplying the junk knows the user is really hooked, the customer will pay a very high price for a fix. Mind you, addiction merely means that for the addict heroin is as necessary as breathing, and probably more so than eating. This means the addict will have a very inelastic demand for the product, and the demand will become less and less elastic (less response of quantity demanded to price changes) as the addiction becomes worse. In fact, this is the economic indication of the phenomenon of addiction. You want the stuff regardless of price and cost. The drug methadone is a partial substitute for heroin. There is some evidence that the use of methadone may be less damaging and less addicting than heroin. There is some reason to believe that this drug can be used to obtain withdrawal from heroin. What has this to do with the market? Some communities have made it relatively easy (cheap) to obtain methadone as part of a supervised program of heroin withdrawal. Economically, the price of a substitute (methadone) has been made cheaper which, hopefully, will reduce the *demand* for the given good, heroin. Notice, another element in the prices of the two goods has also been made cheaper. The methadone treatments have been *legalized* while the heroin use is still illegal. This is a major factor in weighing *total cost*, since the heroin use could involve the cost of imprisonment or heavy fines as well as the cost of the drug itself. Economics, you see, involves costs and benefits beyond those of the immediate market.

Interfering with the Market—Even from the discussion thus far, many of you will be able to figure out what effects could be expected if you prevent the market from operating. Governmental and private bodies continually attempt to control prices in many ways and for many different reasons. Some of these reasons seem quite humane and "socially desirable" on the surface, while others are obviously the work of "vicious selfish dogs" whose only goal is to make a buck and take the public. Let's look at some of these attempts and see if the results, regardless of the motivations, are all that different.

To begin with, return to the case illustrated in Figures 7.1 and 7.2. Figure 7.1 illustrated the case of a price in the market that was "too low"—too low in that an economic shortage existed. People's willingness and ability to purchase exceeded other people's willingness and ability to produce and supply. In Figure 7.2, the price rose under the stimulation of the shortage, and quantities supplied and demanded were brought into equilibrium. What would have been the results if the price had not been allowed to rise?

I teach at an urban university that has had a monumental parking problem. Tens of thousands of students, faculty, and staff move to and from the campus every day. Public transporation, as so often is the case, stinks. Many people live beyond practical walking or biking distance, particularly in the cold winter. For a long time, there was a great hue and cry about keeping the parking fees *low*. After all, the argument ran, it is a student *right* and a faculty *right* to have reasonable parking facilities available. Maybe so, but the point was that the facilities *weren't* available. The taxpayers of the state disagreed with the position of students and faculty about their "rights" and, through their representatives, the public refused to use *their* resources to subsidize the parking requirements. In effect, we had the situation of the quantity demanded exceeding the quantity supplied because the university-established price was below the free market equilibrium. Because of this situation, the price mechanism no longer rationed the supply of parking spaces. What did, then? Very simple. The old principle of the "fustest with the mostest" took over. If you really wanted to be sure of getting a spot, you arrived at 7:00 a.m. Of course, your classes or office hours might not start until 10:00 a.m., but if you really wanted the spot, you got there early! There were a few spots that carried reservation tags. If you bought a permit, it entitled you to use a particular spot, and no one else was allowed to use it. The price of these permits was also well below the free market equilibrium and, again, the allocation could not be accomplished by the market alone. Lining up for permits at the beginning of each year took care of part of the shortage. While I never knew about it directly, it would not have been surprising if another very common allocation mechanism had come into the act—the *black market*. The way this would have worked is that a bunch of enterprising students or faculty members would have gotten in the lineup for permits, obtained them at the *ceiling price* (the artificial price below equilibrium) and then sold the permits to others who had not been willing to spend their time in the lineup. Of course, most governing bodies who set ceiling prices generally frown on this kind of behavior—usually to the extent of making it illegal. In other words, the government adds the additional cost of fine or imprisonment to the black market operator.

The problem, of course, is that not only does the artificially low price leave the allocation of parking spaces up to other means, but also, the low price provides no incentive for anyone to really do anything about the basic problem—too few spots. In this case, there is a reasonably happy ending. The university *did* raise the price of parking; the existing spots were purchased by those who were most willing and able to give up resources for them; and more important, the fees were then sufficient to construct additional parking facilities. I have purposely chosen an example which involved a monopolistic seller (the university) and competitive buyers (the faculty, staff, and students) to show that market restrictions work the same way in a strictly competitive market operating freely or a semi-controlled market such as this.

One or two more points ought to be mentioned. First of all, it is perfectly true that *for those who got spots*, the ceiling price was a bargain and "helped" them by reducing the resources they had to pay for parking. But the hooker was that not everyone was helped. There were those—and "those" were many—who were unable to obtain spots at the bargain price. That group had to go without. Another point that is bound to be raised is that "free" pricing by supply and demand would have meant that the rich old full professors got the spots and the poor starving students who couldn't afford it lost any hope of being able to park. First, this wasn't the way it happened to work, but even had it been true, there would have been another way to handle the problem. All the university would have had to do was to cut the full professors' salaries by some amount (in effect, tax them) and transfer this buying power to the students. Of course, the students might decide to use this extra buying power for something besides parking, but at least the "equity" which they had complained about would be taken care of. They would have had their chance to spend the tax receipts on the parking place, and wouldn't have been handicapped by their low relative incomes. The point is that the free market is very efficient in allocating scarce resources. It provides a truly democratic way for people to decide just what they want most and what they are willing to give up. If the problem of unequal buying power comes up, there are better ways of handling the issue than by trying to fix artificial prices.

On the other side of the coin, various attempts are made to establish floors on the prices in some markets. In the last few years, there has been a great hue and cry about the plight of migrant workers in this country. One of the instruments which has been used to increase wages of field and harvest workers has been the *boycott* of whatever product was involved. There has been a grape boycott, a lettuce boycott, etc., etc. The idea has been to force the growers to meet the demands of the workers by ruining the market for the growers' products. This is an interesting piece of economic reasoning, and it assumes that the *profits* in growing fruits and vegetables is so high that the growers can be forced to give the workers a "decent" wage without raising prices or curtailing production. Unfortunately, such facts as are available do not seem to bear out the assumption. Increasing costs have forced many growers out of business and even if *all* the profits of the remaining producers were spread among the field hands, their wages would still be pitifully small by most standards. Be that as it may, boycotts have contributed toward forcing growers to *bargain* with labor groups, and these bargaining sessions *have* raised wages in some instances.

There, it's just as simple as that! The growers are finally being forced to pay a "just" wage by the collective power of the workers. But those growers have done something else as well. Many of them have reduced their employment of migrant workers. Before, you might not have liked the wage, but generally you could get a job. Now some of the workers are getting jobs, but others are unemployed and, *because of their low level of marketable skills*, they are unemployable. By establishing a minimum wage (price of labor above the market equilibrium wage), some workers gain. But at the high wage, the quantity of labor that people are willing and able to supply exceeds the quantity of labor employers are willing and able to hire. Unemployment is bound to occur.

The boycott can be particularly vicious since it tends to *decrease* the public's demand for the product which will *decrease* the price people are willing and able to pay for the product. This decreases both the profit of the growers *and their ability to pay wages*—certainly *higher* wages. What is the answer then? First of all, the *basic* reason that migrants receive low wages is that the *general public* is neither willing nor able to pay a high enough price for (literally) the fruits of their labor. The value of their product is relatively low. The basic requirement for correcting this situation is raising the skill levels of these people. This can be done by various programs of job re-training, vocational education, and even general education. Fine, but how about the old people who probably wouldn't be able to acquire these new skills fast enough to do any great amount of good? Here again, it depends on what society wants to do. There are plenty of subsidy programs around which can be used to transfer buying power from one group (tax them) and turn the buying power over to another group (subsidy, welfare payments, etc.). Some of these are more efficient than others and will be the subject of further discussion in Part IV. But again, the one thing that is crystal clear is that monkeying around with the *market price* will have some very undesirable side effects that are often ignored. You may hurt the very group that you're trying to help—or at least a large part of that group.

A final restriction that is often placed on a potentially free market deals with quantity limitations of one sort or another. Up to this point we have discussed what happens to *quantity* when there is a change in the *price* of a good. As you might suspect, the relationship will work the other way, too. When restrictions are made on market quantities, there are pressures exerted on prices that must be reckoned with. For example, during prohibition the sale, production, consumption, or possession of alcoholic beverages was illegal. There was still plenty of booze around, but quantities were below those that would have existed under a free market. Quantity supplied was forced by restrictions to be less than free market equilibrium quantity. There was an economic shortage in the same way that there would have been if a *ceiling price* below the free market equilibrium *price* had been established. The tendency is to raise the price people are willing and able to pay for the restricted quantity. At the same time, the artificially high prices stimulate *some* people (those who don't care about the law) to produce like crazy.

In such a situation, how will it be decided as to who will be able to sell their products and who won't? Well, of course, the police help this problem somewhat by cracking down on the illegal producers. An obvious strategy is to try and get the police to crack down on other producers, but to leave you alone. This is precisely what did happen during prohibition, and the police pay-off was very common. It's quite probable, however, that the police won't be able to handle the job alone, so the next step is to try and organize the producers to limit their output to the point where the entire group of producers can make the most money. To do this, the group might well organize their own "enforcing" department. This was done during the prohibition period, and the enforcing by this group was considerably more effective than the police effort. If an uncooperative producer appeared, he was shot. It was a simple and highly effective method.

The same kind of problem exists today in the control of illegal addictive drugs by organized crime. Our laws set the stage for a highly profitable production and distribution system by persons willing to live outside the law. Addictive drugs have the other characteristic of encouraging the giving away of "free samples"—particularly to the very young—to develop future customers. The law sets the stage, and economics predicts the obvious results.

Questions and Problems for Chapter 7

1. List three or four activities that you enjoy doing and for which you have to pay something—not necessarily money, but giving up something else you like. Imagine all things being held constant except the price of doing that activity. Now ask yourself how much of the activity you would "consume" if the price increased. How about the quantity you would demand were the price reduced?

2. Some of you are working. If so, would you be willing to work more hours if your boss were willing to increase the wage somewhat? If he were to double the wage? How about a fifty-fold increase in your hourly wage? For those of you not working, what kind of wage would it take to get you to do some particular job for which you have the skills (or lack of skills)?

3.   If the increased wage rate in question 2 made you "rich" (whatever that might mean), would you then be willing to work more or less for the same wage rate?

4.   List three or four pairs of goods that *for you* are substitutes. Remember, they don't have to be *perfect* substitutes but merely provide some similar services. Think of what your buying pattern might be if the relative prices of each pair changed significantly.

5.   As in question 4, do the same thing for goods which you tend to consume together, that is, complements.

6.   Think of three or four "fad" items that you have purchased during the past few years. Before the fad, what was your willingness to purchase these goods? How much were you willing and able to pay? During the fad? How about now (past-fad)?

7. Have you ever changed jobs voluntarily? What made you change? Can your reasons be put in terms of a change in cost/benefits? Did the market wages of the two jobs reflect these different cost/benefits (to you)?

8. Have you ever been willing and able to purchase something but found that you had to wait "your turn"? Would you have been willing to pay a somewhat higher price and not pay the additional cost of waiting?

9. Using a Venn diagram, show the situation that existed in the 1950's when the federal government assured farmers a market price for some products much greater than the free market equilibrium price. Even if you know nothing about farm policy in the 1950's, you should be able to predict the outcome of this policy.

10. List a few items which you or your family purchase which you consider to be "necessities." For any given percentage change in price, would the quantity you demand change a great deal of a little? Go through the same exercise for some goods you consider to be "luxuries."

No basic presentation of the economic facts of life today could possibly be made without a discussion of environmental quality. We've been talking about economics as the science (or art) of choosing between scarce resources. There are probably no choices that are more difficult to make than the ones concerning the junk that's left after we get through using something. Hard choices *must* be made, however, and mankind is reaching the point where it no longer can be up to Joe or Charlie, the electric company or the paper plant. Each of us has to shoulder at least that portion of the problem to which we contribute. But shouldering the problem won't help much if we don't understand its dimensions and the many potential impacts of both the problem and its resolution. This chapter is intended primarily to start you thinking along lines that may be new to you.

Man, more than any other creature, makes a substantial impact on his environment. Because of his intellect (or in some cases because of the lack of it), he is able to take from nature many raw materials and convert them into things of greater use in satisfying his wants. This is just repeating what was said earlier. Man desires *production* because in this way he can increase the availability of goods from which he derives desired services. We all live on a single mass roughly the shape of a globe. Until recently, man could neither enter this world (except by new birth) nor could he leave it. (Perhaps some "soul" or spirit left, but the physical body merely changed form. Ashes to ashes and dust to dust.) Even today, space travel is a long way from the point which will allow any mass migration from Mother Earth. In spite of the achievements in space travel, the environment we have is the only one we're likely to have in the forseeable future. From a technological standpoint, the desirable situation would be to have all of man's activities result in both *products* and *by-products* which could be re-used or changed into other useful forms without overwhelming expenditures of other resources. Ideally, we would like to live in the world illustrated by Figure 8.1a. In this world, resources are taken from nature and converted into useful goods by some production process. The process creates goods *and crud*, but the crud goes through a conversion process (either natural or man-made) and returns to nature as another useful resource or, at least, as a substance which won't hurt anything. Next, man consumes the product. This results in increased utility or satisfaction, but also produces some measure of crud. In this illustration, this crud also is converted into a neutral form or provides a resource for something else. As long as resources of some sort exist, the closed system can continue to operate. Actually, the basic requirement for the system is the availability of *energy* in some usable form. Without energy resources, the entire system grinds to a screeching halt in very short order. With sufficient energy, almost anything else *can* be accomplished.

The problem arises when the nice regenerative world of Figure 8.1a turns into the crud-producing world of Figure 8.1b. In this case, some or all of the waste goes into a "sink" or reservoir and accumulates. In fact, the accumulation may start a cycle all its own, in which case crud is generated from crud, which generates more crud. In this case, the "natural" cycle or *ecosystem* is disrupted with possibly serious effects for man and nature. So much for the "technical" side of pollution; how do you do something about it? This is where economics comes into the act.

First of all, why does pollution take place at all? The primary reason stems from the ability of some operations to avoid paying all the costs involved in a production or consumption process. Take the example of the electric plant using coal as fuel for its generators. Presumably it will try to maximize profits, but it usually must justify every cost to some kind of public utility commission. It must also *sell* its product, which means that the price of the electricity must be kept within some kind of limits. In any case, if the company can use some resource without having to pay, it will do so. Similarly, the customers of the electric company will be much happier to pay *less* for their product rather than *more*, everything else being equal. They might be willing to pay something more if they realized that the increase would reduce pollution, but without that direct connection, the lower price is certainly preferred. Given this circumstance, the electric company will use, *and maybe overuse*, the free input. In this case, the free input is the ability of the air to carry waste products away from the plant. If the company were paying for the use of the air to get rid of its waste, they would tend to *economize* on the air's use just like they would for any other input that they had to pay for. If they could be made to pay for *all* the cost created by dumping the smoke into the atmosphere, they would cut down the dumping to a point which would no longer be objectionable. This doesn't mean that there wouldn't be any smoke, but anyone suffering from the smoke would be "paid off" to the market value of the damage they were willing to accept. The real problem occurs because

Figure 8.1
Material Balance and Imbalance

a.

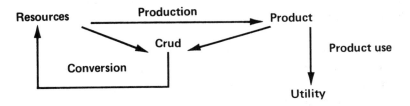

b.

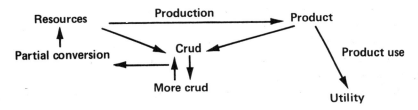

an accurate reflection of all of the benefits and damages in a freely operating market is difficult, and sometimes impossible. We have been emphasizing the point that the market does nothing more than transfer *property rights* from one entity to another. There was even an example that illustrated how exchange becomes meaningless if the property rights can't be defined or enforced.

What are the pollutable resources about which the community is primarily concerned? True, we have *land* pollution and *noise* pollution, but certainly most of our concern lies in the quality of the *flowing* resources—the *flowing* water and the *flowing* air. Who holds the rights to these resources? This is a very good question, but the answer or answers are not so simple. One can say that air and water are "common" property but this doesn't mean much unless the rights of transfer, use, *and restriction from use* are definable and enforceable. In the case of air and water, this is extremely difficult and therefore extremely expensive. The information, contractual, and policing costs of transferring air and water rights can be so high as to make the operation of a market impractical. Think of the air over the building in which you are now sitting. How can you identify *and establish control over* the particular particles that make up that air at that moment? Without building a structure around that air, you just can't do it. True, you can establish control of the *space* in which the air moves, but the air itself is pretty hard to capture and control. I can sell the "air rights" over a piece of ground to someone, but this is simple because the space *is* and will always *be* directly identifiable by identifying the ground under it. This same problem exists to a slightly lesser degree when talking about flowing water. Specific rights over specific units of flowing water are very hard to define and, hence, are hard to transfer.

Some people think this is not really important since what we're worried about is damage caused by pollutants in the flowing resource, not the resource itself. This may simplify some pollution issues, but not many. If there is a single smoke-producer in a given area, and it can be proven that smoke is the cause of some particular damage, then the smoke-producer can be nailed under most property laws. But what if you're in a city and there are a hundred smoke-producers? For the law to do you any real good, you're going to have to prove (1) that damage exists, (2) that the damage is caused *only* by smoke, and (3) that the smoke originated at some specific plant which you can then sue. That threefold task is very difficult. This is only one example of the many problems of property rights and pollution. Let's turn now to one of the solutions proposed by certain groups in most communities of the world.

For lack of a better term, I will call them the "naturalists." Their basic theme runs something like this. Man is basically "bad" in that he messes up the world around him. Any kind of productive activity tends to be bad because it, along with the goods it produces, adds to the mess. The *first* thing that must be done to stop the pollution problem is to cut back or stop economic growth. A return to the simple life with simple values is in order; in fact, if we don't do that we're all doomed to die in our own filth.

Now, this may be somewhat overstated, but the idea of economic growth *necessarily* being a bad thing finds a lot of support in the naturalist crowd. Let's look at this proposition from the standpoint of fact and analysis rather than emotion. First of all, to *control* pollution, it is necessary to expend resources. Cleaning up the environment *or* maintaining a clean environment will not be free. Cleaning up involves *explicit* expenditures on control devices. Maintaining a clean environment involves either control devices or the *opportunity cost* of *not* using air and water for *any* waste disposal. Either way, a cost is there whether the naturalists like it or not! Economic growth, by definition, means that more products are available to the community. Increased economic activity *can* cause more pollution if nothing changes. But increased availability of goods also means that the opportunity is there to use the increased goods for *pollution control. This* use of the increased output will depend on the will of the community as expressed through the market and/or its government. How would one expect the community to "vote" on the use of increased levels of production (income)? Remember when we were talking about superior and inferior goods? Inferior goods were those which suffered a *loss* in demand as incomes increased, and superior goods were those for which quantity demanded *increased* as incomes increased. Would you expect pollution *control* to be a superior or inferior good? To answer that, let me give you an example from a previous generation.

During the Great Depression of the 1930's, there were so-called "company towns" in which there was basically one factory or employer on which the entire economy of the town was based. Many days, the people of the towns would wake up, and the first thing they would do is look out their windows at the smokestacks of the mill. If the air was clear and clean, they were sad, because it meant no work and no dinner on the table that night. On the other hand, if great quantities of black filth were belching forth, this meant work that day, pay that afternoon, and food that night. Environmental quality was certainly preferred to environmental filth, but not if the price was not working and not eating. It is only after necessities are taken care of—necessities as viewed by the members of the community—that great concern over pollution and its control will take place.

What I'm saying, of course, is that pollution control is a strongly superior good, and economic growth means higher incomes. This means that people will be *willing* and able to spend more of their resources on beautiful and healthful surroundings than would be the case *without* economic growth.

Finally, from a practical standpoint, it is unlikely that you are going to be able to convince people that the simple pastoral life is for them. People in most parts of the world are still clamoring for *more*, not fewer, economic goods. Our greatest hope lies in developing a technology that will allow pollution control at a cost the world is willing and able to bear. Here again, economic growth has always been an essential pre-condition to technological progress. When growth stops, technological innovation tends to cease as well.

There is a brief example from the "real" world that sums up the main points I'm trying to make. A local electric company that uses fossil fuels in the electricity generating process has released some rough figures on electricity production and smoke pollution. Since I am basically a skeptical person, let's assume that the company is lying through its teeth. Assume that the figures are off by several times. Even so, the figures are impressive. In the period between 1945 and 1970, this company's output of electricity went up five times. For every kilowatt hour they produced in 1945, they produced five in 1970. At the same time, the amount (*total*) of particulate material (hunks of crud) that they spewed into the atmosphere was *reduced* by 95 percent—not reduced per kilowatt hour, but reduced in total. Maybe the five percent still coming out of the stacks is "too much." Whether it is or not, increased output in this important kind of industry—power production—has not been followed by increased pollutant loadings. Economic growth has produced a technology capable of reducing this type of pollution while increasing output. True, there is more to air pollution than merely particulate matter. There are a lot of different gases which have effects that we still don't completely understand. There is a great deal to be done to improve control, but don't assume that cutting economic growth is automatically going to do the job. It won't—necessarily. Economic growth by itself won't do the job either—necessarily. But economic growth provides the basis on which our choices as a people are expanded. We *can* choose more goods and more *pollution*, but we also have the choice of using our increased affluence to clean up our own mess.

There are many proposals around for getting people to pay the total cost of what they do. Taxes of one sort or another are often mentioned. As an example, if the cost of cleaning up non-returnable glass bottles is so many dollars, impose a tax on the sale of non-returnable containers which will provide sufficient funds to clean them up. Of course, this means that the customer who is very careful about properly disposing of the bottles will bear the same tax cost as the bum who heaves the bottles out on the highway. Another suggestion is to outlaw all non-returnable containers. This might work, although the cost of enforcing a law requiring people to return *returnable* containers might be very substantial. This sort of law might also reduce the incentive that currently is stimulating research in the potential recycling of the resource—cheaper non-returnables.

It has been suggested that rights to air and water for use in waste disposal should be auctioned off to the highest bidders, and the moneys gained used for pollution control. This sounds particularly appealing since it is generally agreed that these resources *do* have the ability to properly dispose of some level of certain wastes. This ability should be used just like any other resource. It is when the resources are *mis*used and *over*used that we have problems. Again, however, the business of controlling what is being auctioned presents the same old problem. How do you define the rights and enforce what has been sold or not sold? There are ways of monitoring emissions and the resulting condition of the air or water being used. These methods are *not* free, however, and policing costs loom large in such a plan.

Another suggestion is to subsidize producers for using and/or developing pollution control devices. This, too, requires monitoring and continued control to assure compliance with the subsidy agreement. The plan also raises the issue of who *should* pay for the control. Should the owners of the companies, their customers, the public at large? These questions have no "right answers" outside of your own beliefs and values. But the questions must be answered nevertheless.

At this stage of the game, you are probably thoroughly confused and wondering what the answer is to the whole mess. Well, "the" answer doesn't exist! Each case of pollution has associated with it a set of conditions, both technological and economic. Solutions will probably come from a combination of policies tailored to the individual situation—at least I hope so. If some general policy is adopted in an attempt to control all pollution, such a policy is bound to fail in most instances. The most basic answer to pollution control is the *willingness* and *ability* of all members of the community to "pay the piper." *How* the piper is paid, and *by whom* are important questions that need answers. But everyone's willingness and ability to tackle the problem is the first necessary condition for success.

Questions and Problems for Chapter 8

1.   Discuss the implications of a law which simply said, "All pollution of water, air, and land must cease day after tomorrow." How would this law affect your own consumption patterns? Do you think such a law could or would be enforced?

2.   If you were able to use a car at no cost to yourself (other than the time you spent) and/or at no cost to your parents, would you use the car more or less? Would this cause more or less pollution? (Be careful! This is a loaded question.)

3. Do you think cars in metropolitan areas have increased or decreased pollution compared to metropolitan areas of the 1880's?

4. If you owned the air around the house in which you live and could identify and legally nail any polluters, would you insist on pristine purity for your air? If a potential polluter owned and controlled the air around your dwelling, would you be willing and able to pay him something to reduce pollution levels?

5.   Check with some smoke-producing company in your area. Do they have any methods of removing particulate matter (bits and pieces of dirt) from the smoke? Do they use water to accomplish this? What do they do with the water?

6.   List the packaging materials used in your home which are generally "one-shot" items. Can you think of any economical way to re-cycle any of these items? Are you willing to carry a brown paper bag back to the supermarket every time you shop? Is your mother or sister willing to do so? How about your father?

7. If someone offered you $1.00 each to return empty beer cans, soda cans, bottles, etc., to the store where they were purchased, would you do so? If someone charged you $1.00 for each can or bottle that was not returned, would you return them? Would it make any difference to you which method was used? Would either method be easier to enforce in general?

8. For those of you who are working, would you take a pay cut to see pollution levels reduced in your own area? In another area? Anywhere in the world? How much of a cut would you accept?

9. Why do you think that *general* concern for environmental quality is a phenomenon of the last couple of decades? There are several reasons, so think of as many as you can.

10. It has been said that the ultimate pollution is man himself, and that the most serious pollution problem is the population explosion. Comment on this proposition.

PART THREE
You in the Marketplace — Tomorrow

"I wish I had the time." "A stitch in time saves nine." "The time was when . . . ." "A time to work and a time to play . . . ." What is this thing called time? Why does the economist talk about it? For the next three chapters, we're going to spend *time* talking about *time*. Once we've spent it, we will never be able to get it back. It will be gone, and there is no known way to recapture that particular time slot. This, of course, is one of the main characteristics of time. It cannot be stored or truly "saved" for another day.

Time cannot be "sensed" in the usual meaning of the word. You can't feel it. You can't smell or hear it. There is generally a realization of its passing, but sleep or unconsciousness can distort the awareness of time. Time really sounds like strange stuff for an economist to worry about. The economist is supposed to concern himself with things like money and material goods. What could he possibly say about something so fleeting and intangible? Plenty!

Time is a concern of the economist because, for most men under most circumstances, time is a scarce good. A good? Indeed, a good! Man derives services from the utilization of time. In general, men are prepared to give up something in order to get the use of this commodity. There you have it. Time is an economic good because it *yields services* and *is scarce*. If it is scarce, there must be some kind of limitation on it, some *constraint,* which makes people willing to give up other resources for its use. Time in the abstract meaning of the term may be infinite; time in a personal sense is limited. There are only so many hours in the day, the month, the year, a particular lifetime. For the individual, time is limited and must therefore be allocated between different potential uses. What are these uses?

Actually, we can define three specific uses for anyone's time. Many of our activities fall into more than one category for any given moment, but the categories are conceptually different. First of all, time can be spent in *working*. We're going to talk about working in a special way. Work will be taken to mean activities from which a person derives the *potential to consume*. In most cases, this will simply mean the thing that he does for a living. The job for which he is paid is the simplest example of economic work. The payment received makes consuming other things possible. The do-it-yourselfer discussed earlier in the book uses his time for two purposes. He is producing something of value *to him* which will replace his having to buy the finished product in the market. Additionally, assuming he enjoys the work, he is gaining *leisure* from the operation. Leisure is the second thing that time can be used for. Leisure is the time that we use to *consume* the things we've acquired. You've probably never thought about it exactly that way, but this is precisely what leisure is all about. Even if leisure is spent just doing nothing, the ability to do nothing and still stay alive generally means that we're using up something earned before—the food that maintains our bodies, the roof over our heads, etc. Finally, we must spend time maintaining ourselves. We must sleep, at least a little. We must eat. Both of these activities may yield pleasure as well, but at times they are carried out because life requires it. Maintaining the various goods that we have, the washing machine, the automobile, and all the other goods which help us do our work and/or bodily maintenance, also requires time—*maintenance time*.

As you can see, all of the time we have can be split into one or a combination of these three functions. A typical human being will spend some time working, some time maintaining himself and his personal capital, and some time enjoying the consumption of the things he has. Figure 9.1 illustrates this point using a pie diagram. The whole circle represents the available time in, say, a twenty-four hour day. The mix that anyone adopts will vary, but as more time is used for one purpose, something else must give. We are all *constrained* by the clock.

This situation is of particular interest to an economy which is producing large quantities of goods and services. There is some reason to believe that someday man might be able to supply *all* of his material wants with such little effort that, for practical purposes, material goods become "free." The point has been suggested that at this moment the economic problem will disappear. Scarcity will no longer exist. Even if this utopia comes about, man will still face scarcity—the scarcity of time. As long as man wishes to live, the scarce item will always plague him. Time is the one economic good which has existed since man came on the face of the earth, and it is the one thing which will remain an economic good as long as man himself is around. True, if everyone decided to commit suicide, then time presumably would be a negative good. Like pollution, man would be prepared to pay something to get rid of life itself. While time wouldn't be eliminated, the individual's awareness of it would probably cease.

One important aspect of time that has been sadly neglected by economists is so-called *free time*. Free time *isn't*! Because time is scarce, people will never be able to get out of some kind of alternative cost when they use time for *any* purpose—including loafing. In this same vein, consuming things *takes time*. It's fine to talk about getting a new set of golf clubs, but they won't do you a bit of good unless you can take the time to *use* them. You may be able to afford the price of a trip to the Caribbean, but can you afford the *time* required to take the trip? Consumption of anything *always* takes time, so even the enjoyable acts of consuming are not without their costs.

There is a particularly excellent work on the subject of time in our contemporary world, and it can be easily comprehended by students using this text. The book, *The Harried Leisure Class*, was written by Dr. Staffan Burenstam Linder (Columbia University Press, New York, 1970). It is really worth your *time* to read it.

There is yet another allocation of time that must be made. So far, we have discussed how time is allocated in any brief period like an hour or a day. Should I use the next moment for work, leisure, or maintenance? There is another whole set of choices that must be made, decisions regarding work, leisure, and maintenance *over* time. How am I going to plan my working lifetime? Should I work like crazy now, and retire early; or should I have a ball during my younger days and "pay it off" by working longer in my lifetime? A similar question is *when* do I wish to consume something? Do I wish to consume the fruits of my labor as they accumulate? Will I "save" some of these resources now for consumption later? Finally, should I borrow all I can now, spend it all now (spend more than my *owned* resources), and worry about paying it back in the future?

All of these questions boil down to how time is to be allocated between *now* and the *future*, and *what* mix of work/leisure/maintenance is to be used *when*. We're merely adding another dimension to the decisions discussed in the beginning of this chapter. It is as though the simple pie diagram of Figure 9.1 was stretched from a flat two-dimensional pie to a long cylinder (Figure 9.2). The length in this case represents our lives over time, from now until the end of our planning horizon. This is not necessarily our *death*, but rather the point in the future beyond which we have no interest *now*. Of course, as life progresses, that planning horizon approaches our own conscious or unconscious estimate of the end of our lives. When we're very young that planning horizon may be that day, infinitely far away, when we enter kindergarten, or graduate from high school, or finally get the Ph.D. dissertation completed. Things that might happen beyond our planning horizon, by definition, do not affect our *present* decisions and therefore are not very interesting.

In Figure 9.2, the use-of-time mix labeled "now" will probably change as time goes on. Some of the changes we can anticipate right now. Others that will take place are not anticipated now. The most usual change is for the work segment to become larger as we pass from childhood into our working lives. Later in life, more time is spent on leisure and consumption while less is spent on working. If ill-health also comes with age, more time will be spent on maintenance. Our *expectations* of the future have a great deal to do with how we act *now*. If you were in the military service, a war was going on, and you were about to be assigned to the front lines, your attitude toward spending your paycheck or putting it in a savings account

Figure 9.1
24 Hours (One Day)

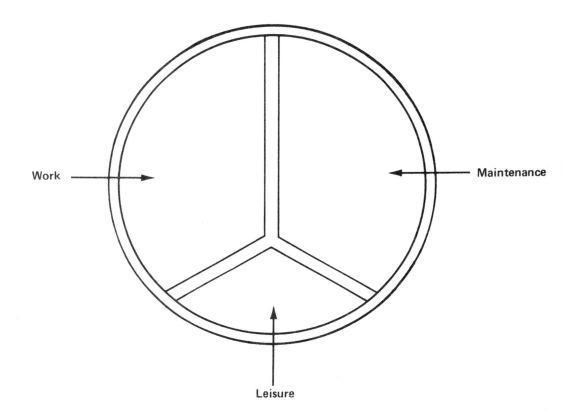

Work

Maintenance

Leisure

Figure 9.2
Time Marches On!

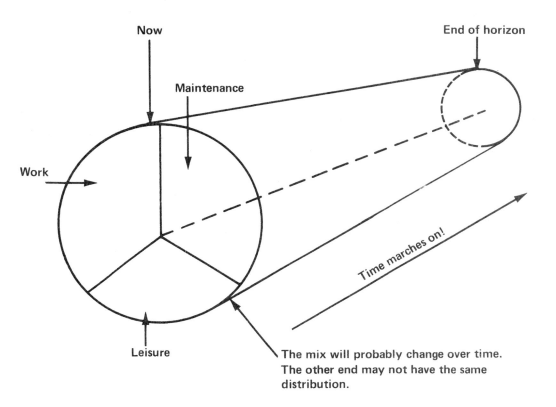

Now

End of horizon

Maintenance

Work

Time marches on!

Leisure

The mix will probably change over time.
The other end may not have the same
distribution.

would be one thing. If you were planning to get married next year and all was peaceful in the world, your decision about spending versus saving would probably be quite different. As you will see in Chapter 12, sometimes people's expectations have a major impact on what actually happens! This can be most important to someone who is trying to guess what's going to happen next in the economy.

Most people prefer their cake now. If they have a choice, they prefer having control over some resource beginning now, rather than sometime in the future. Of course, this makes perfectly good sense. If I own or control something *now*, then chances are I can own or control the same item tomorrow, and the next day, and the next day, etc. If the choice is between this and taking control sometime in the future, I would be foolish to take the future deal unless there was some sort of consideration for doing so. The future may or may not work out the way we plan, but the point is that the future involves some measure of *risk*. It may not be very large, but it exists. *Now* is for sure. Now plus one minute is less sure. Now plus a year, or ten years, is even less sure. *Time* introduces uncertainty into the act and uncertainty means that, everything else being equal, people prefer *now* control over goods to *future* control over goods. Of course, it isn't *just* uncertainty that makes this so. For most people, *present* consumption is preferred to *future* consumption so, again, future goods would not be as valuable as present goods.

All the above discussion is saying is that we tend to *discount* the value of future things. You are all familiar with the idea of a discount and it's not much different here. If you go into a store that's having a sale on shirts, and you find a $10.00 shirt *discounted* by 5 percent, it means that you will pay $9.50 for the shirt instead of the original price of $10.00. It is the same shirt, but its market value is discounted by 5 percent. The same sort of thing occurs with a discount over time. You might be willing (and able) to pay $10.00 *now* for a $10.00 shirt *now*. However, if you had to pay *now* and get your shirt *a year later*, you would probably be willing to pay a lesser amount. For example, you might be willing to pay $9.50 now to get a $10.00 shirt a year from now. You would be discounting the value of a good to be delivered one year hence by 5 percent. As most of you have probably guessed, this discount business must have something to do with *interest*, and indeed it does. Interest is the mirror image of this discount business. Interest is the price we pay (actually, or as an opportunity cost) for consuming *now* rather than waiting until sometime in the future. Of course, if we're *savers* instead of *spenders*, then interest becomes the payment we receive for *giving up* consumption now and waiting until sometime in the future to consume.

The cost of the future is the subject of the next chapter. We will look at both the business of future values, and also at some of the costs of *hedging* the uncertainty of future events. Interest and insurance is the name of the game.

Questions and Problems for Chapter 9

1. Take each of the activities in which you engage now during a twenty-four hour period and classify each as either maintenance, work, or leisure. What is the total for each category? Think back to your routine of five years ago. Again, add up the total for each category. Has there been any change in the mix during the last five years? Think about what you may be doing five years hence. Again, do you expect a change in the mix of your time usage?

2. If, all of a sudden, you were able to take a perfectly harmless pill that would remove your need for sleep, how would you use this extra time—or would you still prefer sleeping? If everyone else in the world also took this pill, would that change your answer? If so, how?

3.   For a man earning $50,000 per year, a one-month cruise costing $1,500 is not exorbitant. What other costs must he consider?

4.   What major expenditures do you presently think you will be making in the next ten years? How do you expect to pay for them?

5. Comment on the economic significance of the phrase, "A stitch in time saves nine."

6. Discuss the probable cost/benefit analysis of the future made by someone about to commit suicide.

7.   What does it mean to "waste time"? Do you enjoy wasting time? Why or why not?

8.   "Time is money." Comment on this statement—*after* reviewing the beginning chapter on money and its functions.

9.   Compare the concept of "time" with the concept of "space." What are the similarities and differences as far as costs and benefits in your life are concerned?

10.   Do you want to live forever? Why or why not?

10. Tomorrow's Pricetags — Interest and Insurance

Happy indeed is the man who can say, "I don't owe anyone anything!" He can further assert that the only interest he is worried about is the interest *received* by him from various loans he has made to others. As far as his having to bear an interest cost, this is ridiculous. He's never paid a cent of interest in his life and isn't about to. Our "happy" man is making a king-sized mistake if he feels this way. Like everyone else, consumption or purchase of a good *now* means that those funds (resources) are not available to loan out. Every purchase *now* cuts down the amount that could have been loaned and for which interest could have been earned. As stated in the last chapter, interest is more than the money you have to pay out to borrow funds. Interest is the cost of buying goods now rather than waiting. One "pays" this cost as an opportunity cost every time one buys a non-interest-paying good of some sort. Time is valuable. Time in the future is worth less than time in the present. As a result, everything we consume now *costs* us not only *what* we consume, but also the amount someone would have *paid* us to forego consumption now.

Interest is a particularly interesting kind of price. Generally, interest is expressed as a *percentage* of the value of whatever one borrows. For example, if one borrows $1,000 for one year, interest—the price of borrowing in order to consume or purchase *now*—would probably be expressed in terms of a percentage of the amount borrowed. If the *interest rate* was 5 percent per year, then at the end of the year, the borrower would owe the lender the original amount of the load—$1,000—*plus* 5 percent of the principal amount—$50. To have control over $1,000 worth of goods and services *now*, I will have to repay $1,050 one year from now. Again, notice the other side of the coin. If one possessed $1,000 now, he could either spend it, or loan it out (assuming, of course, that someone else was willing and able to borrow it). If he spends it now, he will get $1,000 worth of goods and services. If he loans it out, and if he waits one year, he can gain control over $1,050 worth of goods and services. Therefore, if he spends it now, he *foregoes* the interest of $50. The true cost of the *present purchase* must include an allowance for the interest foregone because of spending the money now.

The amount of interest paid or received on a loan will depend on the *interest rate* and the time for which the money is loaned. From the example above, assume that at the end of one year, the borrower pays the lender the interest of $50 but continues to hold the principal amount of $1,000. At the end of the second year, he again would owe the $1,000 plus the interest for the second year—another $50. As long as the lender was willing to have his $1,000 outstanding, the borrower could continue to pay *just the interest* of $50 per year. The amount of the loan would not change nor would the interest due each year.

Now try another possibility. Assume that at the end of the first year, our borrower doesn't pay anything. He still owes the lender $1,000 principal, but he also owes the $50 interest as well, for a total debt of $1,050. If this debt continued without payment, at the end of the second year interest will again be calculated. In this case, however, interest will be computed *not* on the original $1,000 but on the $1,050 that has actually been owed for the preceding twelve months. The interest charge for the second year will be

5% (.05) times $1,050 equals $52.50.

If the interest and principal is again left unpaid, at the end of the third year interest will be calculated on a principal amount of $1,000 + $50 + $52.50, or a total of $1,102.50. Now the interest for year three will amount to

5% (.05) times $1,102.50 equals $55.125.

This process is called *compounding*. The phenomenon of compound interest is very important when talking about choices made between different time periods. As an example, assume you were to continue the process above for a period of forty years. Let's say you put your money in a savings account when you are twenty years old and leave both the principal and interest to accumulate and be compounded each year. At 60 years of age (40 years later) your $1,000 will have grown to $7,039.94. This illustrates how important it is to make sound investments of a long-term nature, particularly if getting your investment out (selling out or collecting the loan) is difficult. We'll be talking more about this in the next chapter when we discuss human capital.

In your everyday life, most of you will come up against many different situations in which you will probably have to pay interest in one form or another. It is important that you realize the differences between these different forms of interest payments, and we'll spend a few minutes looking at some of these forms.

Many of you will probably buy a house some day. If you're like most Americans who buy houses, the purchase will be made by a combination of a *down payment* plus a real estate mortgage on the property itself. The amount of the down payment will depend on many things, including lending laws at that time. The down payment generally must come from your own resources which have been saved or accumulated over the years. Say for the moment that you are going to buy a $25,000 house and you will need a down payment of 20 percent. Your down payment, therefore, is $5,000, and the balance left to be financed is $20,000. Generally, loans that are *secured* by real estate are made with payments calling for *simple interest*. This means that the interest you pay will depend on the amount of your unpaid balance and the length of time the unpaid balance exists. To simplify our example, assume that the mortgage calls for 20 equal payments of $1,000 each. The first payment will be due exactly one year from the date of the loan, and each payment after that will also fall at one year intervals. Generally, mortgages call for payments each month rather than just once a year. You'll see this in the next example. For now, however, let's look at the loan and what it will cost.

On the first anniversary date of the loan, you will have had the use of the full amount of the loan, $20,000, for one full year. Assume that the interest rate called for by the mortgage is 6 percent per year (per annum). Therefore, on the first anniversary, you will owe the lender $1,000 in principal plus .06 X $20,000 ($1,200) in interest for a total payment of $2,200. At the end of the next loan year, you will have had the use of only $19,000 for the preceding year. Therefore, your interest will equal .06 X $19,000 ($1,140). Notice, the amount of interest is $60 less than the year before. The reason is that you are paying interest on $1,000 *less* than you did the year before. That amount ($1,000) times the 6 percent equals the missing $60. The third year, you will have had the use of only $18,000 for the twelve months, therefore your interest will be .06 X $18,000 ($1,080)—again, $60 less than the previous year. As you can see, simple interest means that you pay interest *only* on the actual amount of money you *still owe*, not on the amount of money you originally borrowed.

Figure 10.1 shows a schedule of payments for a mortgage I owe on my house. Notice, at the end of December 1971, the balance owing is $8,940.69. The payment due on the first of January 1972, like each other payment on this schedule, is $175.00. This is a 7 percent mortgage, and the interest portion of the 1 January payment will amount to $52.15. This is obtained by taking the balance remaining *before* the payment ($8,940.69), multiplying it by the annual interest rate (7 percent or .07), and then dividing this amount by twelve to get one month's interest. This means that $52.15 is going to be taken out of my payment and applied to *interest charges*. The balance of $122.85 will be applied to the payment of principal. Therefore, principal will be reduced from the $8,940.69 figure to $8,817.84. On the first of February, the interest will be only $51.44 because I've only had the use of $8,817.84 instead of $8,940.69. Therefore, more of my $175.00 payment will be applied to principal payment ($123.56). By the time the first of October rolls around, only $45.55 will be required for interest and $129.45 will be left to pay principal that month. With an *amortized loan* like this, monthly payments will have a high percentage of interest payments in the early periods of the

Figure 10.1

COMPARISON OF SIMPLE AND ADD-ON INTEREST RATES

Add-On Rate	Simple Annual Interest Rate Equivalent			
	1 yr.	3 yrs.	5 yrs.	10 yrs.
4%	7.30	7.51	7.42	7.11
4-1/2%	8.21	8.41	8.29	7.91
5%	9.10	9.31	9.15	8.69
5-1/2%	10.00	10.20	10.01	9.46
6%	10.90	11.08	10.85	10.21
6-1/2%	11.79	11.96	11.68	10.96
7%	12.68	12.83	12.50	11.69

Figure 10.2

MONTHLY PAYMENTS WITH SIMPLE INTEREST

Payment Date	Amount of Payment	Principal	Interest	Balance Due
				$8,940.69
1/1/72	$175.00	$122.85	$52.15	$8,817.84
2/1/72	175.00	123.56	51.44	8,694.28
3/1/72	175.00	124.28	50.72	8,570.00
4/1/72	175.00	125.01	49.99	8,444.99
5/1/72	175.00	125.74	49.26	8,319.25
6/1/72	175.00	126.47	48.53	8,192.78
7/1/72	175.00	127.21	47.79	8,065.57
8/1/72	175.00	127.95	47.05	7,937.62
9/1/72	175.00	128.70	46.30	7,808.92
10/1/72	175.00	129.45	45.55	7,679.47

loan. As time goes on and payments are made, more of each payment will be applied to principal because the interest charges become smaller.

Remember that one of the reasons that interest exists is to pay people for some risk. If I borrow $100 from you to be paid back in one year, you are taking several risks. One of these is that I might run off to Brazil and leave you with an IOU for the $100, but nothing else. You wouldn't be able to get at me without spending a great deal more than the amount of the loan. Another risk is that I might die tomorrow without leaving sufficient resources to repay the loan. Here again, you'd probably lose your money. Also, I might lose my job tomorrow and be absolutely incapable of paying the money back. There are several things you can do to reduce the risk that exists for lenders. The most obvious and most common is to place a *lien* on some property that I own. This means that something of value that I own is pledged as security for the payment of the debt. In the case of a real estate mortgage, the property that is purchased is pledged as security. This merely means that if the borrower *defaults* (doesn't make) his payments, the lender can claim title to the property. In actual fact, the lender has to go through quite a bunch of legal actions before he can get title to the pledged property, but he can get it, at least to the extent that he recovers the value of his loan. A mortgage, therefore, tends to reduce the risk that a lender takes in making a mortgage-secured loan.

Another way that lenders can protect themselves is with a *contract sale*. Many consumer-purchase items are bought on contract sales. In this case, the seller (or lender) keeps the title to the property until the loan against the property is paid in full. The refrigerator would remain the legal property of the department store until the store is paid in full. Sure, the buyer can use the appliance, but if he misses many installment payments, the store can come and collect *its* property. Legally, it is much less messy to use a conditional sale or contract sale to maintain security over payment of the debt. The seller can repossess the property with much less legal hassle than is the case in a formal mortgage. As a consumer, however, your property rights are much more carefully protected in most states with a mortgage as opposed to a contract sale. As consumers, you probably would prefer to get loans without all of the terms and conditions associated with liens. However, if such liens did not exist in some form, the risks of loaning funds or resources would be increased. This most assuredly would increase the interest rates lenders would insist on getting. In this sense, liens can help consumers by lowering their borrowing cost.

Another form of interest in our economy is a *discount loan*. Here the lender agrees to loan you, say, $1,000 for one year at 5 percent. Under simple interest, this would mean repaying him the $1,000 plus $50 interest at the end of one year. A 5 percent discount loan, however, means that the lender takes his interest off the top at the beginning of the time period. You borrow $1,000, but the lender keeps $50 out of the loan itself. You get $950 to use for one year, *not* $1,000. In addition, you have prepaid the interest, which again tends to raise the real cost of the loan. In our example, you lose the opportunity cost interest on the $50 that is prepaid. Five percent of $50 equals $2.50. In addition, the $50 interest payment was effectively for $950 rather than $1,000. Your interest, paid and foregone, thus totals $52.50 for $950 for the one year period. This comes to a simple interest equivalent of ($52.50/$950 equals) 5.53 percent—over 10 percent higher than a 5 percent simple interest loan.

Finally, we come to that great American institution, the "add-on" interest loan. Most of the installment loan purchases that are made in this country involve this kind of interest. It sounds perfectly simple and reasonable. I want to borrow $1,000 at 5 percent for three years with monthly repayments of sufficient size to pay the thing off. So I go to Friendly Clyde's Loan Company, and he's more than happy to accomodate my desires. It works out something like this. Since I'm borrowing for a three year period, I will pay 3 years times 5 percent or 15 percent for the whole period. That seems reasonable enough, so we'll take 15 percent of $1,000 ($150) and add it to the amount of the loan. Now we have a debt of $1,150 to be repaid in 36 E-Z monthly payments. In addition to effectively pre-paying the interest costs, the real problem comes in that you aren't borrowing $1,000 or $1,150 for *three years*. You're borrowing *this* amount for one month *only*. After your first payment, you'll have repaid some of the principal as well as some of the interest and the amount of the net loan is reduced. But you're paying prepaid interest *as though* you still owed the entire principal amount for the entire three year period. Figure 10.2 shows some of the comparisons between the add-on rate of interest and the simple rate of interest for various combinations of rates and time.

There is another characteristic of consumer loans like this that isn't generally known. If you sign this "contract" you agree to make monthly payments of so much *each* month and *every* month until the debt is paid. Since you are a frugal soul and get some kind of a windfall during the life of the loan, you decide to make a couple of extra payments early. After all, paying early should get you a little rebate on some of the interest, right? Wrong! Most loan contracts of this nature in most states of the nation will *not* give you any credit whatsoever for early payments *unless* the early payment involves complete early payment of the debt. If you want to make an extra payment or two, put the money into some fairly safe investment like a savings account. It won't earn you much, but it will earn you something. When your extra payments thus accumulated are enough to pay off the balance of the indebtedness, pay the whole thing and you'll get some credit on the interest you've already paid.

The truth-in-lending law that was passed in the late 1960's was designed to force lenders to state the *simple interest* equivalent of whatever interest scheme they were peddling. In part, the law succeeds, although things like the opportunity cost on prepaid interest are certainly not included. Whatever the law does or doesn't do, it probably adds to the costs of doing business for the lending institutions. The increased paperwork and clerical time undoubtedly add something, however small, to the cost of doing business. Once again, information is useful, but supplying or obtaining it can be expensive.

One other point before leaving the subject of interest for a while, don't get the idea that just because a 5 percent add-on interest loan turns out to be an 8 or 9 percent simple interest loan, that the interest rate is necessarily too high. That may or may not be the case, but it is entirely possible that 10 or 12 or 18 percent may be a valid market rate for the kind of loan involved. Also, that 10 or 12 or 18 percent *market* rate of interest may turn out to be only 4 or 6 percent under circumstances of inflation in the economy. We'll be talking more about that in Chapter 12.

Insurance is one way that people decrease the uncertainty about the future. When I drive home tonight, there is a possibility I may have an accident. I don't *know* whether I will or not. Tonight, when everyone in the country goes to his respective home, there will be so many automobile accidents. This figure can be estimated fairly accurately, particularly if we talk about the number of accidents in a year rather than on a specific night. Let's say that for a given year we have 100,000 cars in our state. Further, we estimate that there will be 10,000 automobile accidents with and average cost of $500. If I am an "average" driver in this "average" year, then my chances of an accident are one in ten. Now, if every driver in the state pays a $50 per year fee, the dollar value of the total fees will equal the dollar value of the accident costs. If everyone agreed to do this, then the costs of all the accidents could be paid by the fees, and no one person would have to bear the cost of any single accident. Obviously, this assumes that the collection of the fees and the transactions cost of paying for the accidents do not involve expenses. They do, in fact, involve considerable expense, so a pro-rata share of these would also have to be added to the fees collected for the scheme to be self-supporting. Also, differences in the drivers might be translated into higher or lower rates for specific groups because of differences in the loss experience of the separate groups. But notice just what this idea accomplishes. It takes a comparatively large, *possible* cost in the *future* and converts it to a much smaller *certain* cost *now*. This is what the insurance game is all about. Many people would prefer to pay a small known cost in the present to prevent the *possibility* of having to pay a large cost later.

Even in the field of life insurance, this same situation holds. Everyone is going to die sometime. On the average, men will die at a rate of so many for each age group in any given year. Pure life insurance, straight *term* insurance, merely pays a present sure cost for the possibility that you will die earlier than the average. If you don't die earlier, the company will make out. If you do die earlier, the company will lose on *you* (but never on the group as a whole, assuming their tables are accurate). The actuarial tables used by all insurance companies are based on the past experience of the community concerned as to what people, or groups of people, die when. If life expectancies are *increasing* while the charges for life insurance are based on worse experience (old tables), then the insurance business is going to do very well indeed. On the other hand, if experience is getting worse than the actuarial data being used, companies can get into trouble very quickly. The first type of experience has characterized the life insurance business in many periods of our history, while the latter problem has occurred in automobile insurance. During some periods, experience in auto accidents has gotten worse than preceding periods upon which charges were calculated.

What about insurance, life insurance, as an investment? Well, if you want a fairly low risk investment with very little effort required on your part, things like *ordinary life insurance* may be okay for you. The returns to this kind of investment are low when compared with alternatives of similar risk levels. The main point to remember in looking at life insurance programs is to sort out the true *insurance* costs and benefits from the investment costs and benefits. This gives you some basis on which to make your decisions.

Questions and Problems for Chapter 10

1.   Assume a man holds all of his assets in cash. If price levels fall, will he be better off than he would have been by investing in other goods whose price is falling? Explain your answer.

2.   As a project, go to a finance company, a regular bank, and a credit union and compare the actual interest that would be charged by each one on an eighteen month installment loan to purchase a $3,000 automobile. Are the down payment requirements different? Is there a realtionship between the down payment and the rate of interest charged? Is there a relationship between the amount of down payment and the company's willingness to make the loan? Are there "hidden charges" such as additional required insurance, closing costs, service charges? How about penalties for early payment (do you get all your prepaid interest back)? How about late payment charges if you miss a payment?

3. Go to a local life insurance agent and have him explain just what you are paying for under different programs of life insurance. Ask (insist) that he show you the actual cost of the life insurance itself under each program. Ask him to show you the actual rates of return on the investment portions of the programs. Based on an average rate of inflation of, say, five percent per year, what has been the true rate of return on these investment programs through insurance?

4. Why do interest rates tend to be slightly lower on home mortgages with large down payments than on those with comparatively small down payments?

5.   Why do "loan sharks" (individuals, mobs, or companies) do most of their business among poor people? Think of some ways that might help low-income people obtain credit. The obvious suggestion is legal action, but see if you can get at some of the basic problems in this area.

6.   Why does General Motors Corporation generally qualify for the lowest rates of interest while middle-income citizens generally pay more?

7. What do you think would happen to interest rates on consumer purchases (washers, dryers, ranges, refrigerators, etc.) if conditional sales were eliminated and title to the good was transferred before the debt was paid?

8. What interest rate would you be willing to pay if someone were willing to loan you one million dollars? What would you do with the money? (Assume you had to pay it back.)

9.   What rate of interest would you need to be persuaded to loan one half of all the money you receive from any source?

10.   Although the answer to this question will be covered specifically later on, what do you think high interest rates would do to help stop inflation?

There are several titles that could have been put on this chapter, but "getting productive" seemed to be about as descriptive as anything else. What we'll be talking about is how and why man developed *tools*—tools in the broadest sense of the word. Instead of calling these helpful instruments tools, people usually refer to them as *capital.* Most of you have probably heard the word "capital" used in many different ways. "I would like to buy that thing, but I don't have any capital." In this case, the speaker is probably referring to lack of money or lack of other assets that could easily be converted into money. You may have heard stocks and bonds, or perhaps a savings account, referred to as capital. We will be using the word in a much broader sense. Capital will mean *anything* created or developed by man to assist him in the general process of production.

Some kinds of capital are very tangible. Machines, buildings, roads, and dams can be seen; their contribution to productive processes is also visible. Less obvious but equally productive are "investments" made in human beings through education, health programs, etc. There are important differences between investment in non-human and human capital, but there are also many similarities. Let's look first at some of the general characteristics of all capital.

If something is produced for use as *capital,* it usually means that the same item cannot be used for consumption purposes at the same time. Since, by definition, scarce resources are used in the production of a capital good, then something is being created using resources that *could have been* put to work in producing something for *direct* consumption. The point is that to get any capital goods, *consumption now* must be foregone by someone. As covered by the discussion of interest earlier in the book, if a market system is used, then people must be given an incentive to forego consumption—a *market* incentive. This incentive is a *return* on any *investment* they make. The return must reimburse them for the postponement of consumption plus reward them for any risk they might be incurring. A return on an investment is generally in the form of interest paid on that investment. If you *loan* someone $100 now, you expect him to repay your principal amount at some time in the future *plus* a return on this investment of *yours* in the form of interest—a percentage of the principal amount for every unit of time (per month, per year, etc.). As long as you value the interest you can get *more* than the return you could have gotten by using your money in another way, you will make the loan. If the return (psychological or monetary) you would get from a new dishwasher costing $100 would be larger than the return you'll get from the borrower in the form of interest, then you would buy the dishwasher instead of lending your resources.

In this simple example, one can see the entire rationale for investing or not investing. It falls in with exactly the same pattern that man follows in making any decision between alternatives. One looks at the alternatives and weighs the *total* psychological and monetary benefits involved. One then chooses that course of action(s) which produces the highest *net* benefits.

Another example is one that you may actually face someday. With the advent of leasing plans, one doesn't have to buy an automobile anymore to get the services of an automobile. Instead, it is possible to rent or lease a car over long or short periods of time. How are you going to decide which to do? Should you buy a car, or should you rent one? First of all, I'll assume that whether you own or lease makes no difference as far as non-monetary considerations are concerned. In other words, the fact you *own* the bucket rather than lease the machine won't *by itself* make any difference. You're not willing to pay one penny for the prestige of either owning or leasing. In this case, the choice can be easily made by adding up all the costs of buying and operating your own car and by comparing these costs with the costs of leasing or renting. If owning comes out cheaper, you'll buy; and if renting comes out cheaper, you'll rent. Of course, particularly when you calculate the costs of ownership, be sure you include *all* the costs. For example, if you plan to keep a car two years and then trade it in on another one, be sure to estimate the difference in the price you pay for the car and the price you will receive for it two years hence. This difference is called depreciation and, particularly when it comes to automobiles, it can amount to a very substantial sum of money. Another point just in passing— cars don't depreciate the same amount each year. Most of you probably realize this all too well. The cost of depreciation on an auto during the first year of its life will be much greater than the second year. Similarly, the second year's depreciation will be greater than the third year. Beyond that, it is more difficult to generalize. But understand that the market for cars places a considerable premium on their use during the first couple of years.

There are all kinds of examples which most of you either have faced or will face shortly. How about the decision to buy a washer-dryer versus going the laundromat? In this case, you will probably have to put some kind of value on the time spent going from home to laundry and back. You may even have to include the cost of babysitters if you have small children at home. All of these these potential costs and benefits must be tossed into the calculations before you can decide whether it is better to *invest* in some appliance or to rent the services of it. Many of you won't even worry about it. The time and effort needed to figure out these kinds of things may be more valuable if used in another way. It may be just too much trouble to figure it out. Fair enough, but realize at least that you may pay a *price* for the luxury of *not* figuring out such alternatives.

Investment decisions made by businesses are very similar in their motivations to those of individuals. The cost and benefits of different alternatives are estimated, and the cheapest alternative is chosen. This may not be the cheapest for *today* but rather over the long pull. An action (including an investment action) will be taken if the cost of doing it is less than the money it will bring in. If the *income* derived from some action is greater than the *cost* of taking the action, then the company's profits will be increased. In the business world, this is the name of the game. Profits are to be maximized. Interest, either that actually paid on borrowed money or that which could be earned on the company's own resources, is the cost of investment. If the expected return from the investment exceeds this cost, the investment will be made. This means that high interest rates will tend to cut down on investment, and low interest rates will tend to increase investments. This is absolutely correct, again, on an everything-else-being-equal basis. From the *cost* side of things the statement is true. Of course, often high interest rates are also associated with periods of high potential profits. Even paying high rates of interest will still produce profits, and investments will continue. Conversely, low interest rates may well exist in times of economic slowdown where potential profits are low. In this case, investment may not take place in spite of the low cost of borrowed resources. Like any other situation in life, you can't look solely at the *benefits* or solely at the *costs*, but you must look at the *net* between any particular set of benefits and the particular set of costs that go with those benefits. Whether the result is net profit or just net satisfaction for an individual, the *net's* the thing.

We have already discussed briefly why people tend to specialize in their activities. Without at least some capital, this specialization can't go very far. There is only so much that can be done "by hand" without the aid of any tools whatsoever. Man's material progress has been the story of his accumulation and use of capital. All men have become "capitalists" in that all men in all types of economies employ at least some capital. The first thing the Russians did after the revolution was to begin a hard program of *forced* capital development. It is only recently that consumer goods industries have really become a major part of the Russian economy. Regardless of the methods used, they were absolutely correct in realizing that any great material progress in the country would depend heavily on having the capital needed for production. Our own history is the same in this regard. All of America's economic growth has taken place because of heavy portions of her output going into capital formation.

On a practical note, if one has a few extra bucks around, how can he invest them? What sorts of alternatives exist for investors today—particularly small investors? This book is most certainly not designed to be a small investor's guide to fame and fortune. Very briefly, however, let's mention a few of the alternatives you might have.

First of all, there is always the savings account. A so-called passbook savings account has the advantage that, in general, monies can be deposited and withdrawn with little or no notice to the bank or savings and loan association. It has the rather substantial disadvantage that interest paid on such accounts is always comparatively low. Another advantage, however, is that these accounts are generally insured by the government and therefore the risk of loss is almost nil. Variations on the savings account are many and usually involve some kind of commitment on the part of the depositor to leave the funds in the account some minimum length of time. Sometimes the requirement is to give a certain minimum notice to the bank prior to withdrawing the deposit. Often this type of account is called a Certificate of Deposit rather than a straight savings account.

Another possibility for the small investor is the purchase of U.S. government bonds. Always keep in mind that the purchase of *any* bond is merely the loaning of your funds to someone else. The borrower is selling you a peice of paper stating that he owes you so much money at such and such percentage of interest, and that the debt will be repaid with interest at some specific (or in some cases, unspecified) date in the future. This is true of a government bond, a corporate bond, a municipal bond, or a personal bond. Interest on U.S. government bonds is very low compared to other investments. The primary advantage of this type investment is the complete safety of it. As long as the government exists, your savings are safe—at least the *dollar* amount of those savings is safe. We'll talk about the *real* value of investment under conditions of inflation and deflation in the next chapter.

The mention of municipal bonds brings up another point. At the time this book is being written, interest on municipal bonds is exempt from U.S. income tax. Then clearly everyone ought to buy municipal bonds so that the interest earned can be kept without giving any to Uncle Sam. The trouble is that a lot of people have the same idea, and the good old market mechanism tends to make the *return* on these bonds—the interest paid—lower than interest paid on other bonds of similar risk. If you are in a *very* high income tax bracket so that you are paying a very high percentage of every dollar earned to the U.S., *then* these municipal bonds with their tax exemption may really be a bonanza. In the lower tax brackets, the advantage is much less clear.

And then, of course, we have the stock market. *The* stock market doesn't exist. There are several stock markets in this country and many more abroad. Their function is to provide a place where buyers and sellers of *stocks* can get together for the purpose of exchange. To even talk about stocks at an elementary level, we must look at the way businesses are set up, and the way they keep records. In no way is this discussion to give you a knowledge of either accounting or corporation finance, but it should provide enough information to get you started should you wish to continue.

First of all, businesses divide their accounts into different categories. Things which they have certain porperty rights over are called *assets*. Things which they owe other people are called *liabilities*. Things which they "owe themselves" (or own) are called *equities* and *reserves*. There is an identity which by definition of the categories must exist. The value of the assets of a firm must equal what they own themselves plus what they owe others. Assets must equal liabilities plus reserves and equities. There's nothing magic about this. The accounts are set up so that it must be true. This idea can be put into the form of a *balance sheet* which lists the value of all the firm's assets, the value of the firm's liabilities, and the value of their equities and reserves.

Figure 11.1 illustrates a very simple balance sheet for a fictitious firm. The Purple Gunch Co., Inc. had assets worth $175,000 on December 31, 1972. These assets were broken down into *current assets* and *fixed assets*. There is no hard and fast rule as to which is which but, in general, current assets are ones that can be converted into cash very easily. They are very *liquid* or exchangeable. In this case, they consisted of (obviously) cash on hand, money in the checking account, money that is owed by customers and expected shortly (accounts receivable) and finished goods ready for market. Fixed assets are those that could be sold, but over a longer period of time. They are less liquid or exchangeable. For the Gunch Co., this group consisted of the factory and equipment. Under liabilities, again there is a rough distinction made between monies owed shortly (accounts payable to suppliers and short-term notes to lenders), and those monies owed later on. The total liabilities of the company were $20,000. Since the assets were $175,000 and the liabilities were only $20,000, this means that the Gunch Co. was *worth*, on a *net basis*, $155,000. When the company was organized, the original money came from the sale of common stock—$55,000 worth of common stock. Let's assume that this consisted of 1,000 *shares* of stock at an opening price of $55 per share. This, then, is the amount the company owes *its owners*—its *stockholders*.

Obviously, the Gunch Co. has done reasonably well in business and, instead of paying all its profits back out to its owners (stockholders) in the form of dividends or a return on the stock, it has retained these earnings for future use by the company. Nevertheless, these retained earnings are part of what the company owes itself—part of its reserves and equities.

Well, back to the stock market. As you can see, *stocks* are the pieces of paper that represent a share of ownership in some particular company. There are all kinds of common stocks, preferred stock, etc. In all cases, they represent some claim on the assets and/or earnings of a company. The stock markets are places where people can trade these equities.

There are two ways one can make (or lose) money in the stock market. First of all, you may buy a stock because a company is expected to pay earnings on each share, and these earnings would represent a good return on the money invested. It might be considerably more than the *interest* that could be earned on a loan of some type. Of course, the *risk* will be higher too. Maybe the company won't make any money. In this case, they might not be able to pay a dividend (return) on your investment.

Figure 11.1

BALANCE SHEET
for
The Purple Gunch Co., Inc.
Dec. 31, 1972

Assets

    Current Assets

Cash in bank	$ 11,000.00
Cash on hand	100.00
Inventory of finished goods	27,500.00
Accounts receivable	11,400.00
Total Current Assets	$ 50,000.00

    Fixed Assets

Factory and office building	$100,000.00
Machines and fixtures	25,000.00
Total Fixed Assets	$125,000.00
TOTAL ASSETS	$175,000.00

Liabilities

    Current Liabilities

Accounts payable	$ 5,000.00
Notes payable within 6 months	5,000.00
Total Current Liabilities	$ 10,000.00

    Fixed Liabilities

Notes payable after 6 months	$ 10,000.00
Total Fixed Liabilities	$ 10,000.00
TOTAL LIABILITIES	$ 20,000.00
Retained Earnings (Reserve)	$100,000.00
Common Stock Outstanding (Equity)	55,000.00
TOTAL LIABILITIES, RESERVES, AND EQUITIES	$175,000.00

A second way in which money can be made in the stock market is to buy some stock at a particular price, then having the stock *rise* in price, whereupon you sell it and make a profit. It's as simple as that! All you have to do is identify and buy some stock that is going to go up in price, and you've got it made. Aye, there's the rub! What will make the price of a stock rise? In the long run, the ability of the company to make money and pay their stockholders will determine the value of the stock. But that "long run" may be very long indeed, and actual profit-making certainly can't explain many of the rather fast fluctuations in stock prices from day to day or month to month. The fact of the matter is that the largest determinant of stock prices at any moment in time is people's *expectations* of what's going to happen. This includes expectations about the profitability of the company itself, but also expectations about what's going to happen to the economy in general. If the president has a heart attack, the stock prices will probably bounce down because of the *uncertainty* such an event can introduce. If you can outguess the expectations of the entire buying and selling population in the stock market, you can and will get rich over night. If you guess wrong, you can lose your shirt and everything else along with it. In the long run, the general level of stock prices will follow the economic activity in the economy. In the long run, stock can be a safe, sound, and low risk investment—some stocks can be. But in the very short run, making large profits has about the same odds as an honest crap table in Las Vegas. You may win some, and you may lose some. If you're a real expert, your odds may be better, but they're still odds.

Getting into and out of the stock market is a fairly simple operation, and I'll give you a real-life example from my own rather limited experience. On the 15th of March, 1971, I picked up the telephone and called my friendly stockbroker. There had been problems down in Chile about that country's desire to kick Americans out of their copper industry. As a result, the stock prices for copper companies with U. S. mines had been going up. With just a telephone call, I ordered the broker to *buy* 200 shares of Bagdad copper (yes, this is a *domestic* copper company) which was then selling for a price of $28 1/2 per share. The total price of the sale was $5,700 and the brokerage added their commission of $66.50 plus another surcharge of $15.00 to bring the total transaction to $5,781.50. Incidentally, the commission is based on the dollar value of the purchase (or sale) and the surcharge is made *per transaction* no matter what its value. Figure 11.2a shows the confirmation of this transaction that was sent to me by the broker after he made the purchase. According to the rules of the stock exchanges, unless I had a special credit account (which I didn't), I had five days in which to pay for the purchase.

Well, old Bagdad Copper did go up in the next couple days, but not much; and I needed some money for another purpose. So again I called the broker on the 18th of March and told him to sell half of the original purchase—100 shares. Figure 11.2b shows the confirmation of this order. One hundred shares were sold at $28 5/8 per share, making a sale price of $2,862.50. From this gross amount, a $4.50 New York state exchange tax was deducted. (This stock is listed on the American Stock Exchange in New York City.) A surcharge of $15.00 (per transaction) was also deducted along with a $.06 fee which goes to the Securities and Exchange

Figure 11.2

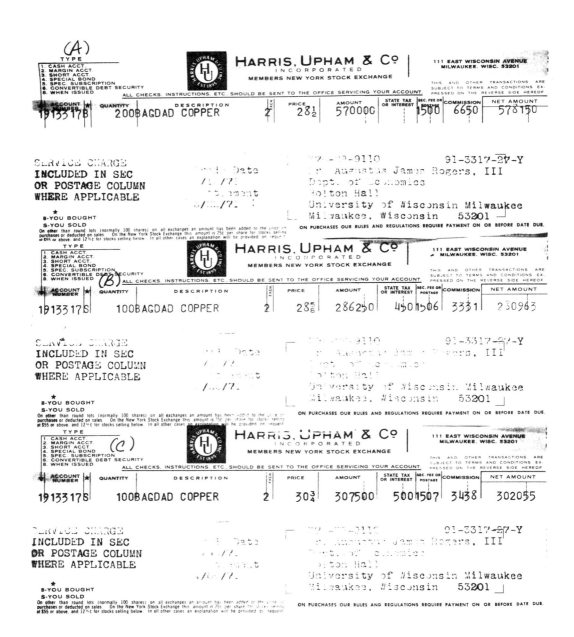

Commission. The broker's commission (they get the surcharge, too) was $33.31, leaving net proceeds on the sale of $2,809.63. Notice, that while the price of the stock when I sold this 100 shares was 1/8 of a dollar ($.125) higher than when it was purchased, I still lost money on the deal because of the transactions costs in both the buying and selling. The total amount I had paid was $5,781.50 for 200 shares, or in other words, $2,890.75 for 100 shares. Therefore, because of the commissions and fees involved in the transactions, I lost $81.12.

At this stage of the game, I decided that if the market for Bagdad Copper got to $30.00 per share, I would sell the other 100 shares. Therefore, I gave the broker a *sell* order for 100 shares of Bagdad Copper at 30. This merely meant that if the market for this stock reached $30 per share, he had an automatic order to sell. A copy of this order is shown as Figure 11.3. At the same time, I placed *another* order with the broker saying that if the price of Bagdad Copper should fall as low as $27 1/2 per share, he was ordered to sell at the best price he could get. The document for this order is similar to that illustrated in Figure 11.3, except that the wording in the body was "Sell 100 Bagdad Copper @ 27 Stop 27 Limit." This is known as a *stop loss* order. Notice that the effect of these two orders was to limit either the losses I might incur as well as the profits. If the stock price moved very much in either direction, I would get out of the market. In actual fact, the market on Bagdad did fall for a few days, but never low enough to cause the stop order to be executed.

After that lousy period, suddenly things began to pick up in the market. My broker called and said he *thought* that probably the price would go quickly above the 30 top I had ordered. I therefore cancelled the 30 sell order, and what do you know. The price went to 30 3/4 ($30.75) where upon I sold it—quickly. The confirmation of this transaction is shown in Figure 11.2c. The gross amount of the sale was $3,075.00, from which the $5.00 New York state tax was deducted along with the $15.00 surcharge, $.07 SEC fee, and $34.38 commission. The net amount of the sale was $3,020.55. Adding this amount to the net amount of the sale of the first 100 shares, I took in $5,830.18. My original purchase of the 200 shares had cost $5,781.50. My net gain on all this was $48.68. The loss on the sale of the first 100 shares was more than offset by the gain on the sale of the second 100 shares. I was lucky—nothing more or less.

If you like to gamble, this kind of very short run trading can be fun, but it is gambling and should be viewed as such. Like any other investment, *potential* returns are going to be valued by the market by the estimated risk involved. The higher the risk, the greater the potential profit, but also the greater the potential *loss*. Remember, the chances are that information you have about expectations is probably available to a lot of other people too. The market is bound to reflect these expectations in the price of the security. A stock may look like a "good deal" because of a low price. But be careful, there is probably some very good reason for that low price. Check it out.

There is one category of investment about which a few special words are in order. We have said that man without any tools is severely limited in his ability to produce anything. This

Figure 11.3

HARRIS, UPHAM & C°
INCORPORATED

111 EAST WISCONSIN AVE.
MILWAUKEE, WISCONSIN 53201

March 18, 1971

AS OF THIS DATE WE HAVE ~~ENTERED~~ FOR YOUR ACCOUNT, THE FOLLOWING ORDERS, WHICH WE SHALL KEEP GOOD UNTIL COUNTERMANDED . IF INCORRECT, PLEASE ADVISE AT ONCE.

```
Sell
100 Bagdad Copper @ 30
```

WHEN STOCKS SELL EX-DIVIDEND OR EX-RIGHTS WE WILL REDUCE OPEN ORDERS TO BUY OR OPEN ORDERS TO SELL ON STOP.

WE WILL NOT REDUCE OPEN ORDERS TO SELL OR OPEN ORDERS TO BUY ON STOP.

YOURS VERY TRULY,

HARRIS, UPHAM & C°
INCORPORATED

PER _____ **RML-27** _____

Mr. Augustus James Rogers III
Dept. of Economics
Bolton Hall
University of Wisconsin Milw.
Milwaukee, Wisconsin 53201

statement is particularly true if we include as "tools" his knowledge, training, education, developed dexterity, or whatever else you want to call developed abilities. Getting these abilities and skills is very similar to making an investment. In fact, economists consider education and training as being an investment in *human capital.* One very big difference between investing in human and non-human capital is the ability to change an investment once made. If you buy a productive machine, and you wish to change it for a different machine, you can sell it and buy the new one. With investments in human capital this is impossible unless we have slavery, and even then reselling the *investment* is still impossible. You might be able to buy and sell the person in whom the investment was made, but *not* the investment itself. If you continue your education and become a history major, once this is accomplished there is *no way* you can sell the investment you have made in that direction. Sure, you can sell the services *flowing from* the investment, *but not the investment itself.* If you find that this particular major was a mistake, you won't be able to trade the resources spent getting that training into resources to obtain some alternative set of skills or knowledge. Once an investment has been made *in a person,* it cannot be retrieved, only *used.*

Why do people get an education? There are many reasons, and not all of them are connected with merely earning a living. But a large part of the reason most people have for getting formal educational training is to improve their earning power. As long as increased training results in a good return on the resources invested in that training, then it certainly pays. If you can earn more from an alternative investment of comparable risk, then that alternative should be chosen, at least as far as the market is concerned. There may be non-market benefits related to your ideas about the "quality of life" that can be gotten from, say, university training. But as far as the ability to gain higher lifetime incomes, the investment in a college education should produce returns at least as high as investments in other comparable alternatives.

Does a university or high school education "pay" in this sense? The answer, in this country at least, is a definite *yes.* Several studies have indicated that resources in high school and university training will produce as high or higher returns to the investor as other comparable investments. This doesn't mean that *all* university programs nor *all* high school programs will pay off. It does mean that, on the average, such an investment is worthwhile.

A few years ago, I did a study of the incomes of high school and university graduates in Brazil. In Figure 11.4, the average earnings of secondary school graduates of different ages is plotted against the earnings of all university graduates in different age groups for the population of Brazil's second largest city—Rio de Janeiro (which is the State of Guanabara). You can see the very substantial difference between the average incomes of these two groups over their lifetimes. Even when the additional cost (or investment) to get the university education is thrown into the act, the return to the additional investment is substantial. In terms of the cost of the university training *to the individual,* one cruzeiro (the Brazilian unit of currency) invested in a university education at age twenty produced a 16.7 percent average return

Figure 11.4
Guanabara—Age/Income Profiles—1960

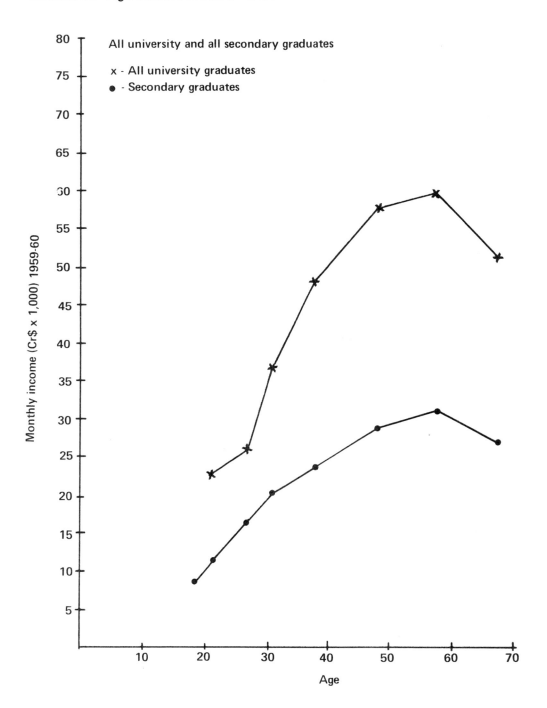

throughout every year the graduate worked. This means that every cruzeiro invested at age 20 would produce 482 cruzeiros by the time the individual reached age 60. Not a bad investment in anyone's book!

Well, summing up this business of getting productive, it will and does require investment in capital which is used to assist the production processes of the economy. To get this capital, present consumption has to be given up. Investments will be made if the expected return exceeds the cost of making the investment. In simple terms, this means that the expected return would have to be greater than the interest rate for loans of comparable risk.

Any investment must return amounts needed in order to induce people to give up consumption to form capital. These amounts are going to be roughly proportional to the overall risks involved. If there is a lot of risk, the return will be higher, and if there are few risks, the return will be comparatively modest.

Now you've seen some of the more important areas of specific markets that *do* and *will* affect your lives. Now it's time to look at the economy as a whole, and how you fit into this enormously complicated world. Again, we will touch only the highlights, but it should help you see how things tend to work.

Questions and Problems for Chapter 11

1. Make a list of the capital goods you own. Remember, anything that assists you in work, maintenance, or leisure without being immediately used up in the process qualifies as capital.

2. If you own a car, sit down and figure out just what the expenses of owning it are. Include an estimate of depreciation, gas and oil based on the number of miles you expect to drive this coming year, a reserve for repairs, a reserve to buy new tires, an item for your own time spent on maintenance activities. Now call two or three leasing companies and get quotes to lease an automobile of approximately the same quality. How much did you save or how much did it cost you to own the car rather than lease it?

3. Do the same thing as in question 2 for a washer-dryer laundry facility. Be sure you include the difference in your own time required for each alternative.

4. Assume that for the average two-pack-a-day smoker, his working lifetime will be cut by ten years. If he admits to this fact, how might it affect his decision to become a Ph.D. or M.D.? Would society be better off to subsidize his education or that of a non-smoker? What additional information would you need to fully answer the question?

5.   Make a list of the risks and benefits associated with each of the following investments: U.S. Savings Bonds, a preferred stock of a major U.S. corporation, a common stock of a major foreign company, a savings and loan company deposit, a time deposit in a regular bank.

6.   Getting your instructor (and perhaps a simple computer program) to assist you, figure out how much you will have to earn over your estimated working lifetime to make your present college or high school education "pay." Use some of the cost figures already calculated from earlier chapters. Use any reasonable rate of interest as the "opportunity cost" of the resources you have invested in education.

7.   Analyze the costs and benefits associated with a publicly financed campaign to treat venereal disease. Think about both the immediate cost-benefits and long range effects.

8.   Draw up a personal balance sheet including a fair market value for all your assets, a list of your liabilities, and your net worth. This last figure could be negative at the moment. While it is seldom done in practice, include the value to date of your educational expenses as an asset consisting of human capital investment.

9. Educational expenses are often subsidized by taxpayers on the theory that society gains more than just the value of the increased productivity of the student. What might some of these "external" benefits to society be?

10. "Eat, drink, and make merry for tomorrow we will die." Discuss the implications of this philosophy.

PART FOUR
You in the Economy

In Chapter 3, we began a discussion of what money is and why we have it. Many of you probably could see even from that discussion that money and the level of prices in any *closed* situation were intimately related. It's almost as simple as the arithmetic. If there are only two goods around, and getting more of one means giving up some of the other; then the *price* of one good is the amount of the second good that has to be given up. If there are five oranges and ten apples available, and that's all there is available—just two goods—then in terms of the available supply, one orange is worth two apples. The price of *oranges* is 2 apples/orange. Can you figure out what the price of apples would be from these figures? Of course, the price of one apple is the reciprocal of the orange price. The price of *apples* is 1/2 orange/*apple*. Now, if the supply of apples suddenly doubled to 20, what would happen to the price of oranges *and* apples? Five oranges are now "worth" (in terms of available supply) 20 apples. One orange, therefore, is worth 4 apples; and conversely, one apple is now only worth 1/4 of an orange. The *price* of oranges in terms of apples has doubled, and the price of apples in terms of oranges has *halved*. This has happened because the supply of one of the two goods has doubled.

Now let's go back to the shopping center example of Chapter 3. As with the example above, everything in our shopping center world will be reduced to either the money we have or a composite group of all other goods and services that are available. This last group of goods and services we will call a market basket. It is the "average" set of purchases that the "average" consumer buys in an "average" time period. As we showed in Chapter 3, if the number of dollars available to buy the existing market baskets *doubles*, then very simply, the *price* of market baskets in terms of the dollars that must be given up will also double. Nothing has happened to increase the number of market baskets. The *only* thing that has happened is that more pieces of paper called dollars are floating around and prices have increased to use up this extra money. If the shopping center now becomes the entire economy, the same thing will hold true. Given some level of production of goods and services and some level of money stocks, people will use the available stocks to buy goods and services (including *future* goods and services through the credit markets). Some *price level* will result that just absorbs the available goods while using the available dollars. Since the production of money is a function of the government, it *can* control the supply of money.

Let's say that everything is going along fine with a constant level of production and a stable money supply. The price level will also stay constant. Now assume the government wants to increase its purchases of the existing goods and services. In fact, it may want a new good or service. Maybe someone decided to heat up a little war somewhere and our government reacts by buying more tanks. If all the resources in the economy are already doing something productive, where are the tanks going to come from? Well, the government might just say that if we offer an automobile manufacturer enough *money*, he'll stop producing some of the automobiles and produce our tanks instead. Nothing could be simpler, and to make it really easy, the government can just print the money needed to buy the tanks. The government *can* and *has* virtually done this on some occasions.

But our beautifully simple world gets complicated. Someone forgets that there are still dollars around that would have been used to buy automobiles, but there aren't as many automobiles available as there were before. Part of the resources that were producing cars are now producing tanks. What are people going to do with these extra dollars? Very simple. They are going to start bidding for the automobiles that *are* still available. This will drive the price of automobiles up. As the price of autos goes up, people shift some of their buying power into the *attempted* purchase of other goods. However, there are no more of these being produced than previously so the prices of these things go up too. The government will get its tanks alright, but with no corresponding reduction of the purchasing power in the rest of the economy. The prices in the economy will simply go up with no necessary increase in the level of production. This is *inflation*. There are more dollars around with the same amount of goods available. The price of the relatively abundant dollars will go down—their purchasing power will go down. This is exactly the same thing as saying that the price of market baskets (goods) has gone up. Inflation is something that can happen only when the available goods become scarcer with the same availability of money, or when money becomes more available for the same level of goods and services on the market.

If this is the case, then it would seem that the government had all the power it needed to control inflation, by reducing or not increasing the money supply. As a matter of fact, that is absolutely true in the long run. The problem comes in that there are some other things that can happen when inflationary forces are around and the money supply *isn't* increased some. We'll talk about that in the next chapter. There is another question you might raise right now. "Why bother about inflation? If all inflation means is that *all* prices, including wages, go up together, then what's the problem? Sure prices are higher, but so are everyone's wages. No one is better off, and no one is worse off. Right?" Wrong. The basic problem is that, in actual practice, not *all* prices change together. When the *general level of prices* goes up, some prices go up more than others and some wages go up faster than others. As a result, some people might *gain* for a while and others might *lose* for a while. If you are unfortunate enough to be receiving a fixed dollar amount every month, and the price (purchasing power) of dollars is going down, you're clearly going to be *worse off*. Of course, if prices were going down instead of up, and you still had the fixed dollar income, you'd be making out very well.

Inflation has a particularly interesting effect on purchases made over time—on borrowing and lending. Let's see how inflation would affect borrowers and lenders. Assume for the moment that I loan you $100 for one year at 6 percent simple interest. This means that you receive enough money *right now* to buy $100 worth of goods *right now* at today's prices. If prices don't change in the next year, at the end of the period you will repay me my $100 of principal plus $6 of interest. I will be able to buy just as much with my $100 as I could have when I made you the loan a year previously. In addition, I can buy another $6 worth of goods from the interest earnings. Now let's take the same loan over the same time period with the same rate of interest. This time, however, we'll assume that inflation—a rise in the price level of things I might want to buy—occurs during the year to an amount of 4 percent. Prices have risen by 4 percent. The price of the dollar (purchasing power of the dollar) has gone *down* by 4 percent. At the end of the year, I can take the $100 you repay me and buy only $96 worth of goods in terms of last year's prices. It will take $4 of my interest earnings just to make up for the loss in value of the money I loaned you. This means the *real* rate of interest I have earned on my money over the last year *isn't* 6 percent, but rather 6 percent minus the 4 percent decrease in the value of the principal—a real interest rate of 2 percent. Who has gained and who has lost? Simple enough. Inflation helps debtors by making the value of what they have to repay *less* in terms of its buying power—less in terms of what they have to forego in order to repay the loan. Obviously, the opposite is true for lenders. They become worse off with inflation since the purchasing power of the money they have loaned *decreases* as the general level of prices *increases*.

During the late 1960's, people were screaming about the fantastically high interest rates in the country. True, the *nominal* rates of interest were steep. Nine and ten percent rates were common, and many times even higher rates prevailed. But at the same time, there was an inflation at the rate of about 6 percent per year going on. What then, were the real rates of interest? Not much more (if any) than in times of relatively stable prices—3 to 5 percent in terms of *actual* interest paid on borrowed funds.

Does this mean that the opposite would be true with falling price levels? Yes, indeed. If prices are falling, borrowers become worse off and lenders are better off. The value in terms of purchasing power of the principal goes *up* as prices fall. The lender will have to give up *more* command of goods and services when he repays the loan than was the case when the loan was made.

When there is an inflation going on, doesn't the market for loan funds reflect this expectation of rising prices? The answer is yes, at least to some extent. Again, we'll use the example of the late 1960's. The nominal rates of interest went up, but much of this increase reflected expectations of higher *and rising* price levels. It was interesting because supposedly the higher interest rate would reduce the *shortage* of loan funds that existed at the time. The shortage seemed to continue, however. The increasing rates of interest barely kept pace with the inflation, and because of the uncertainty that both the inflation and the *expectations of further inflation* produced, investors and lenders did not increase the availability of loanable funds. Of course, some of this was also due to deliberate efforts of the government to reduce the demand for current goods and services—to postpone demand until sometime in the future.

Why would this policy help reduce the upward pressure on existing prices? If people have a certain buying power based on their *incomes* and their current abilities to borrow funds, then their total demand for goods and services will be so much. If something increases their income, their buying power will increase, thus increasing their present demand for goods and services. Similarly, by increasing the *ease* or decreasing the *cost* of borrowing money, demand for goods *right now* will increase. Most people don't borrow money just to put it in an old sock. They borrow money to buy something *now* rather than wait until they have saved enough to purchase it in the future. Increasing the interest rate would tend to discourage borrowing and present spending by making it more expensive. However, if the increased interest rates are offset by inflation, the real interest rates *don't* increase, and there is no cutback in the demand for present goods and services.

Is there any way to "hedge" against inflation? The secret would be to find some good to buy which could easily be exchanged both now and in the future, and whose value will go up *at least* as much as the inflation and preferably more. There is no surefire good like this but often things like land, certain stocks, precious metals, diamonds, or paintings provide goods whose value tends to rise as fast or faster than the general prices rise. Be careful about these generalities. They aren't always correct.

Finally, who pays the cost of inflation? Again, there is no simple, general answer. It will depend on the time and circumstances of the inflation. There have been some recent studies that suggest that recent inflations have tended to redistribute income toward the poorer end of the earnings distribution. The argument runs that inflation means that factors of production are not only *fully* employed, but actually *overemployed*. We are trying to get too much out of too little. However, this situation may give job opportunities to people whose comparatively low productivity would prevent their getting jobs in normal times. Certainly, people who just hold *money* are bound to suffer from inflation. People who hold fixed money-valued assets are also going to lose because the buying power of the money-valued asset will decline—the same old business of the lender losing.

There is no clear-cut statement of whether rich people gain or lose in inflation. True, if people are very wealthy, they can afford better *information* about inflation-resistant investments. The chances are that they can adjust their *portfolios* in such a way as to minimize the impact of inflation on the *real* value of their investments.

As is often the case, the guy who is neither wealthy nor poor—the guy in the middle— probably gets hit the worst by inflation. His investment portfolio isn't sufficiently large to justify a lot of expensive information-gathering. Chances are he'll maintain a savings account in a bank where the real value of his account may easily *decrease* even with the interest paid on it. If the inflation rate is 6 percent, and he is receiving 5 percent interest on the balance in the account, the real value of that investment *plus interest* will decrease by one percent a year.

Questions and Problems for Chapter 12

1.   In recent decades, many Latin American countries have tried to "finance" development by the simple method of printing additional currency to pay the government's bills. Discuss this course of action. Who will end up paying? Can you think of any circumstances in which this method might be partially effective?

2.   Describe the mechanics of inflation offsetting an interest rate. You can almost get this one right out of the text, but it is *very* important that you really understand the process.

3.   When average price levels are calculated, certain specific information is automatically lost. List some of the problems of using average figures such as Gross National Product, Per Capita Income, increased productivity, etc.

4.   If I get more money, I am better off. If everyone gets more money, everything else remaining the same, nobody is better off. Explain this paradox.

5.   For most economic goods, if an economy has more of them, the economy is better off. In other words, if a good yields services, the more goods you have, the more services. This isn't necessarily true for money. Explain.

6.   Consider our economy with *wheat* being used as money. All present forms of money would be made illegal, and only the physical commodity, wheat, could be used. What would some of the problems be? What would be the value of wheat?

7. Now let's allow pieces of paper promising to pay so many bushels of wheat to the bearer to be used in our money system. How would this change the situation?

8. Finally, assume the economy is rolling along and people are using the wheat certificates for money. All of a sudden, all the wheat (not the certificates) is hit by a virus and destroyed. What happens now?

9.   Some societies in history have used wives as a form of money. Discuss some of the problems of this arrangement.

10.   At least one study indicates that the very poor in this country tend to *gain* by inflation. How could this be possible? Under what circumstances could they lose?

From the comments in the last chapter, you might well ask how there can be such a thing as unemployment of productive resources. If the resources are *productive* and available in limited quantity, then the price or wage of the resource should adjust to insure employment. True, if the product of the resource was no longer demanded, then unemployment could exist; but assuming the product *was demanded*, then price would go up or down to bring quantities supplied and demanded into equilibrium. You notice, I've been talking about the employment of resources—factors of production—not just labor, but *all* resources. Unemployment of labor is a concept that is often talked about, and when we talk about the subject of "unemployment," usually it is unemployment of labor that is being discussed. Nobody cares much if a machine is idle or a factory building vacant; but if a *man* can't find work, that's a matter of public concern.

This is probably shortsighted because an unemployed factor of any kind means that something is *not* being produced that *could be* produced. Unemployment of any factor means *waste*; and waste costs everyone including, perhaps, the man who doesn't have a job. Our brief discussion here will concern itself with unemployment of factors of production in general, not *just* unemployed labor.

Before continuing further, let's look at a picture of the whole economy of a country (any country) and how production takes place. For the moment we'll assume that foreign trade doesn't take place. Now we have the same situation we've described so many times. "There ain't no such thing as a free lunch." With a closed economy, any economy, if something is to be *used*, it must be *produced*. Nothing comes out of thin air except the flu, and even the flu bugs came from somewhere. In Figure 13.1a, this system is illustrated. We divide all activities in the economy into *consumption, production*, and *inventories* (stocks of goods for one purpose or another). Consumption activities demand goods and services from the production parts of the economy. These goods can either come directly from the producers, or from existing stocks of goods (inventories). Producers supplying goods either supply them directly to consumers or, again, by way of an inventory of some sort. Now, the consumption sector of the economy also makes up the holders of factors of production. The consumption sector provides the labor and the "saved consumption" (the capital which goes into the production processes). Thus, any economy has a circular flow—goods and services from consumers to producers. Clearly, the functions of consumption and production can be vested in the same person or entity, but functionally they perform in this circular flow pattern.

In Figure 13.1b another flow, going in the opposite direction, has been added to the diagram. Instead of the direct transfer of goods for factors and factors for goods, our old friend *money* comes into the act to simplify all the transactions. Money, therefore, flows in a direction opposite to the flow of *real goods and services*. Again, you can see how price levels will be influenced by the amount of money in relation to the amount of goods. Given a flow of goods to factors to goods, etc., there is no reason to believe that increasing or decreasing the money in the system will change that flow. Sure, *prices* will change since it takes so much money to carry on transactions at any given price level. But if we *reduce* the money in the system, prices should fall so that the smaller quantity of money supports the same level of transactions. In the same way, *increasing* the money supply will simply mean there is more money around to carry on the same level of transactions. Prices will rise to use up the extra dollars.

This brings us to the first major cause of unemployment. All along, we have insisted that quantities supplied and demanded of anything could be brought into equilibrium by price adjustment, and so it can. But the problem comes when institutions and individuals in the system *don't allow* prices to adjust. Let's go back to the simple set diagram used to illustrate the market operation. Our "market" now is the entire economy made up of all the separate, smaller markets for *all* goods and services. There are a lot of problems in arriving at this concept, but most of them will be swept under the table for the moment. Figure 13.2 shows our set of *effective* wants, our apparent willingness and abilities to purchase all goods and services. In Figure 13.2a, the effective supply of goods and services is exactly coincidental with the effective demand, and there is no problem. People can get the goods they desire at the existing market prices, and factors wishing to work at the existing wages can all find jobs. As always, *everyone would like to have more*, but given what's available for both producing and consuming, the price mechanism has allocated the scarce items as efficiently as possible. Now assume something happens to change people's expectations about the future. For a specific example, assume that people think that prices are going to start falling. If this expectation really takes hold in the economy, many people will cut back on their present purchasing in

Figure 13.1
The Closed Economy

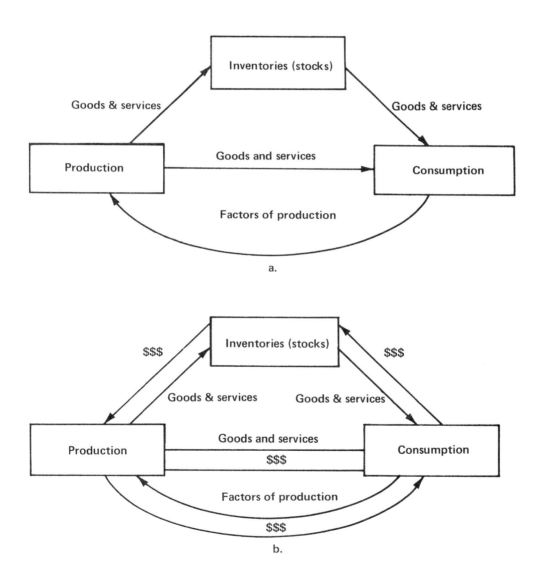

a.

b.

Figure 13.2
Equilibrium and Surplus in the Economy

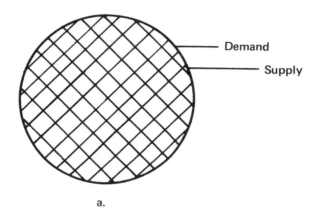

—— Demand

—— Supply

a.

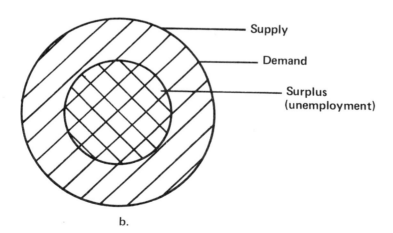

—— Supply

—— Demand

—— Surplus
(unemployment)

b.

hopes of getting the desired items shortly at a lower price. This action will reduce the present demand for goods and services. In Figure 13.2b, the demand has been contracted to less than the available supply. If prices can adjust, they will fall, thus causing an increase in people's demand for goods and bringing about an equilibrium once more. But now assume that prices and wages—at least *some* prices and wages—are not allowed to fall. Assume that some particular union has a contract with industry which calls for a specific *money* wage which cannot be legally reduced. Also, assume the producers have made long-term contracts which protect them from a price decrease in the future. Even the government gets into this act by having long-term purchase and sales agreements that tend to make price movements "sticky"—particularly sticky in the downward direction. Like the minimum prices discussed before, having this kind of floor in the market means that prices *can't* perform the allocation function any longer. There will still be forces that try to bring supply and demand back into equilibrium, but the forces find themselves thwarted when it comes to the price mechanism. Something else has to give. The something else often turns out to be *incomes* in one form or another.

Producers find that they can't sell their products in the quantities they could before. By our assumption, they can't (or won't) cut prices. Therefore, they end up selling *less*. Producers' incomes have gone down, not only their *profits*, but also their total sales which are used to hire factors of production. This means that fewer factors will be hired to produce the restricted output. If wages are also sticky in a downward direction, the problem is further accentuated because the now "too high" wages will also reduce the employment of the factors involved. Incomes of the factors decrease, tending to further reduce the buying power of the consumption sector. This further reduces overall demand for goods and services, which may further depress the whole economy. Notice what has happened. Something that started out as a purely psychological phenomenon—a change in expectations about the future level of prices (or economic activity) actually *caused* the new expectation to occur. If prices had been flexible downward, there wouldn't have been any great problem. Incidentally, prices are *always flexible* both upward and downward, but the problem is how much *time* it takes for the adjustments to take place. The more constraints imposed by price and wage contracts, the longer will be the adjustment period. During the stickiness period, some other factor has to do the market adjusting and, in the case of reduced demand, that other factor is usually *income* and *level of employment*.

What can and should the government do about this sort of problem? The "can do" boils down into two basic tools that themselves are not all that distinct—*monetary policy* and *fiscal policy*. The "should do" depends primarily on your values and what you believe to be the proper relationship between individuals and the several governing bodies. Let's look at the "can do" items and leave the "should do" part for another time.

If our unemployment has been caused by prices not being able to fall, the government can certainly do something to raise the general level of prices back up to its original level: Pump more money into the economy. The actual method of doing this can vary, and the mechanics aren't really that important at the moment. What is important is that the government *can* and *does* control the money supply of the country. If the money supply is raised, the apparent purchasing power of the individuals in the economy is also raised. This, in turn, raises the demand for goods and services. In Figure 13.2b, this would again expand the demand to equal the available supply and eliminate the band of unemployed or surplus resources. This policy might also have considerable impact on expectations since, if people think that prices may be going *up,* this in itself can stimulate present consumption. People now want to buy stuff before the prices rise.

A second general action that can be taken by the government consists of changing the demand for goods and services by changing the demand for government uses. For example, if there is unused capacity in the economy or some segment of it, the government can purchase materials and services from that segment. This will have the same effect as that of anyone demanding the goods and services from that segment—at least, the same initial effect. There are some very important conditions that must be considered in trying to estimate what the total effects of such government purchases might be. First, just because the government buys something doesn't necessarily mean that total demand for goods and services in the economy will rise. Let's say that there are 6,000,000 automobiles being produced and sold this year, but there is still unemployment in the automobile industry. The government comes into the act and decides to increase its purchase of automobiles by 500,000 units and let government workers use these cars for their personal transportation. This will be a new fringe benefit for working for the government. Does the demand for cars automatically go up by 500,000 units? No. Some of the new cars will truly represent an increase in demand, but some of the newly purchased government cars will merely replace or *dis*place previous private sector purchases. Some cars that would have been purchased by government workers for their own use will not now be purchased. Government demand has merely replaced private demand for this bunch of cars. This phenomenon is often overlooked when the results of government actions are estimated.

In a more general way, if the government increases its purchases of goods and services and, to pay for these purchases, raises taxes on consumers, the spendable (after tax) incomes of consumers will be reduced. This reduction in *disposable income* may cut back consumer demand for goods and services and offset the increase in demand produced by the government. Of course, if the government taxes resources that were otherwise being hoarded—not being circulated in ways that create production—then *total* demand would still increase somewhat by taxing and spending by the government. The net increase in demand would come from government use of previously unused resources.

An analogy might be found in the so-called land reform projects of some developing countries. Large tracts of land are either taken (taxed) or purchased from large landholders. These lands are then distributed to small farmers. If there has been substantial *underuse* of the tracts under the original owners, this policy, everything else being equal, can raise production since the small farmers will utilize the resource. Of course, there are several side effects to this particular policy. The new users of the land may be much less efficient than the old ones because of lack of know-how or capital. Also, if the old land was lying idle as part of a comprehensive land-use program that included cycles of non-use for conservation, the long-run effect may be to overuse the resource and ruin it for future generations. No one has siad that any of these factors *are* the case for land reform *or* government policy. Like all other economic policy, the point to remember is that side effects can and do occur. Nice simple solutions to complex problems should always be viewed with skepticism and analysis to attempt to estimate just what may actually happen—not just what "should" happen. There will be more on government finance in the next chapter.

The unemployment of resources discussed thus far has had as its major cause the existence of rigid prices and wages, at least inflexible prices and wages. Another cause of unemployment should be mentioned. This is the unemployment at some moment in time caused by the inability of resources to move. Move in this case refers not only to a movement from place to place, but also movement from occupation to occupation. Our highly developed economy has brought about some tremendous changes that affect this mobility business.

From the standpoint of *physical* mobility—mobility from place to place—rapid and relatively inexpensive transportation has made it possible to move all kinds of resources more easily than ever before. Along with this "small world" created by better transportation and communication, *attitudes* toward moving from place to place have probably become more open, too. Why is this important as far as unemployment is concerned? Demands change for different goods and services. All kinds of changes take place that affect one region's comparative advantage in producing something versus that of some other area. If men and capital can move, then the signals given by prices in the markets can be more easily obeyed. Factors can move into the places and occupations which promise the greatest return for them. Notice, I said *return*, not just money wages. The returns to the factors can include the pleasure of having a California beach nearby, or the mountains of Colorado, or the pine forests of the northern states. Physical mobility increases the ability of man to *optimize* the rest of the choices around him. Basically, it increases the set of choices available.

Unfortunately, our great economic development has been related to another characteristic that has *decreased* mobility between different occupations. When we first started talking about increasing productivity, the business of specialization came into the act; and it has cropped up several times since. It is absolutely true that increasing productivity—the ability to get more from less—requires increasing levels of specialization. Again, I'm not talking *just* about labor—capital items have become increasingly specialized as well. This high degree of specialization occurs in response to a market demand. During the 1950's and 1960's, there was a strong demand for aero-space engineers. These people, particularly after working in the specialties, became very good at their respective jobs, but those jobs had very little direct application elsewhere. In the early 1970's, the demand (primarily government demand) for aero-space products fell off sharply. The rest of the economy was operating at less than full bore too, but when aero-space personnel tried to find alternative employment, the results were very discouraging.

What has happened is that increasing specialization has certainly increased our productive capabilities. But the side effect has been to *reduce* the ease with which changes in occupation can take place in response to changes in the demand for different products. The handyman who was pretty good at fixing the plumbing, painting the woodwork, caring for the garden, and building a kitchen cabinet probably never received as high a wage as the specialist in each of those fields. But if he couldn't find a job doing one thing, there were several other choices available to him. The mastercraftsmen did not have the same alternatives. There is a lesson to be gained from this discussion that should be considered by each and every one of you. As you progress through the various stages of your education and training, keep in mind that there is a "trade-off" between high degrees of specialization in training and a more general education. If you bet right on your specialized choice, you may make it big as far as economic rewards. However, should something go wrong in your employability, you may be in deep trouble. On the other hand, should you choose a more generalized training, you may have more problems getting the best wage—at least until you've gained a specialty on-the-job. However, should you be required to change your entire occupation, you have a base of general knowledge which you can build on. Highly specialized talents are necessary for material rewards, but there is a trade-off in risk that accompanies the rewards. If this last statement sounds like a replay of the statement regarding risks and returns to investment, it's because we're saying the same thing again. It's important.

Finally, this discussion should suggest some public options in solving the problem of specialty-caused unemployment. Retraining can help in many cases to give alternative skills for which a present market exists. Of course, retraining takes *time* as well as resources, and these programs won't be instant successes. Since public resources are involved, there is also the question of who should pay. Again, there are alternatives. If the market really wants the new skill, then it should be possible for the person receiving the training to repay the value of the required resources from the proceeds of his new employment. This idea has a lot of merit in many cases. It has even been carried over into the field of university financing. Several institutions have begun programs of granting very low interest rate loans to students who agree to pay back the total cost of their education from the monies they receive in their future employment. Some plans even offer the alternative of paying a fixed proportion of their future earnings to finance future generations of students. Whatever else, this plan has the merit of making the market reflect educational needs in a more precise way than it now does. If the community wishes to flatly subsidize some person or group, of course it has that option. Then who actually pays depends on who pays the taxes. And on that note let's move on to the next chapter on economics in the government. Notice, I *didn't* say "economies in the government." That's another subject, unfortunately.

Questions and Problems for Chapter 13

1.   What is "unemployment" of a factor? Is a former Olympic runner with a broken leg underemployed? Is a buggy whip factory unemployed if no one wants buggy whips?

2.   Using Venn diagrams, explain what is being attempted when the leaders of a socialist country carry out a propaganda campaign against buying consumer goods.

3. Are "flower people" and hermits unemployed? Are they unproductive? Explain your answers *very* carefully and state explicitly all your assumptions.

4. What occupational specialty are you planning to undertake? What related jobs could you also fill if the demand for your services suddenly disappeared or was drastically reduced?

5.   Explain how willingness to move can be a substitute for multiple skills. What do you think the impact of large families is on labor mobility?

6.   The more flexibility any system has, the more likely it is to be efficient. Discuss this proposition as far as an economic system is concerned.

7. Explain just how rigid downward prices can cause factors to become underemployed or unemployed. Do all factors lose from rigid downward wages? Who does lose?

8. What would be the difference in government expenditures to dig holes and fill them up again as compared to expenditures for a new dam for hydroelectric power? Think this one out carefully. The answers are not as simple-minded as they first appear.

9. List some things the federal government might do to reduce unemployment. What things might a union do to reduce unemployment among its members? What could a manufacturing company do to reduce unemployment of its facilities?

10. What are the similarities between "labor" and "capital" as factors of production? What are the differences? What unique characteristics do natural resources have as factors of production?

Throughout this book, we have made several references to the government (or governments). In this chapter we will combine some of these thoughts plus a few more. Functions that have been covered in some detail previously will only be mentioned, but other functions will be described in more detail now.

The functions a government *should* perform depend on the values and ideals of the community involved. There are still countries in the world today which have almost absolute rulers—rulers who literally can control life and death on a grand scale. In these cases, whatever power other people have is held at the pleasure of the ruler (or ruling group). Other societies have governments with lesser absolute power vested in the top. Still others have ruling elites controlled to some extent by people *under* them—some measure of popular control. Finally, we have representative government in which, theoretically, power is vested in the people, and the ruling group serves only at the pleasure of the majority. In this case, power is supposed to go from the ruled to the rulers.

In almost all cases, there are certain functions that most societies find it desirable to have governments perform. Those that are of particular interest to the economist deal with the establishment and maintenance (enforcement) of property rights. Remember, no matter *whom* property rights are vested in, the rights *must* exist and be effective before any rational attempt can be made to alleviate the whole problem of scarcity. In the free market type of economy, this means that government must lay the ground rules for playing the economic game. This means that it must make the basic laws of property, and the rules governing the transfers of property. As a corollary to this, the governments at the several levels must provide the enforcement mechanisms that will insure the operation of the game according to the established rules. Of course, if there is to be any change, then also the government must have some orderly mechanism built in to allow the changes to take place without completely disrupting the operation of the system. Some societies in which this change mechanism got fouled up found themselves destroyed by violent upheaval instead of orderly development.

Even the market system *can* allow the government other areas of operations if those in the system wish to do so. These other functions generally come into being because of the development of some kind of *market imperfection.* Most of these are caused by an individual or a group getting so much power that they can individually or collectively influence the operation of the whole system for their personal gain. In these cases, it will mean that their gain will be only at the expense of someone else. As an example, during the latter part of the nineteenth century, some industries became very large (for their day) and very powerful (again, for the time). There was strong evidence that because of the development of this power, the laboring classes were not able to get their fair share, to receive the value of their productivity. Early in the twentieth century, the government changed some laws which then allowed labor to organize and become powerful. The idea was that the excess power of some industries could and would be offset by the newly created power of some unions. These two groups started doing their things; it began to look as though somebody would need to protect the little guy who was neither a union member nor a captain of industry. The government was the natural candidate, so big government began to develop, partially to offset the excess power of industry and organized labor. Of course, then the question comes up as to who is going to protect all of us from big *everybody* (everybody, that is, except each of us as individuals). This one hasn't been answered as yet. Actually, in spite of all the power concentrations around, the old economy has managed to survive and produce in fair-to-middling shape. Whether or not you believe in big and powerful governments, you should be aware of several facts.

First of all, the operation of any government involves *costs* to the community. Resources must be expended for the operation of a government as they are for the operation of anything else. Each time a government embarks on a new function, this means more expenditures of resources. It is inevitable, not necessarily bad, *but often overlooked.* We come back to the fact that "There ain't no such thing as a free lunch"—particularly if the government is involved.

Where do governments get their resources? Again, we can make a general statement on this one that has nothing to do with the *kind* of government concerned. The government must obtain its resources either from some body outside of the community (such as payments to Arab sheiks from foreign oil companies), or from within its own community. The universal method of accomplishing the latter is through the imposition of *taxes.*

There are many complicated forms that taxation can take, but generally they can be broken into three types, *taxes on earnings, taxes on purchases,* and *taxes on property.* The first two types involve taking a portion of a flow of resources. Taxes on earnings cease if the earnings cease. Taxes on purchases don't take place if nobody buys anything. On the other hand, taxes on property are taxes on a *stock of value*, and these taxes can continue as long as the stock exists and is owned by someone.

Let's look at each of these three categories in more detail, starting with the income tax. The income tax is clearly an "ability to pay" tax—if you don't earn, you don't pay. It generally takes the form of collecting some percentage of earnings from individuals or companies. If this percentage of tax *decreases* as incomes *increase*, the tax is called *regressive*. People with low incomes will pay a higher percentage of their earnings to the government. On the other hand, if the percentage of tax *increases* with *increases* in earnings, the tax is called *progressive*. The higher the income the higher the *percentage* of income paid in taxes.

The income tax in the United States was designed to be progressive. This means that as one gets into higher and higher brackets of *taxable income*, the percentage of that taxable income paid to the government increases. As the statement is made here, the system works just fine. But if you look at the percentage of *total* incomes paid by different income bracket people, this progressive quality starts to disappear. The present laws allow many deductions from *total income* prior to arriving at *taxable income*. In many cases, very wealthy people are in a better position to utilize the so-called "tax loopholes" than are persons of middle income or low income. The extreme of this can be seen in the fact that there are still tens of millionaires in this country who pay no income tax at all. Don't blame them. They're not cheating (or at least they wouldn't have to cheat) to get this result. It's the way the law is set up, and if society really wants to change it, they can. There is nothing necessarily "better" or "worse" about an income tax over some other kind of tax. An income tax can be made progressive, neutral, or regressive just like any other tax. Although it is sometimes said that an income tax is the only way to get *everyone* to pay their "fair" share, this is not true either. The guy who actually pays a tax is not necessarily the one who signs the check to the Internal Revenue Service.

For example, who pays when the profits (net income) of a manufacturing industry are taxed? Basically, it will depend on the cost structure of that industry *and* the elasticity of the demand for the product. Taxing the industry will raise costs in the industry. Just because the tax is on *profits*, don't think the companies in the industry are just going to pay it and not do anything else. For some, the tax will mean that they can use their resources more profitably in another endeavor. These firms will leave the industry in favor of another one. Production in the industry will therefore decrease. Those that remain in the industry will have to raise the prices they charge for the product, maybe not by the full amount of the tax, but at least by some amount. Prices of the product will go up. People buying the product now have to pay a higher price, and the public at large will be getting less of the item than before.

Who pays the tax? Both the producers and the consumers. The producers pay through increased costs and decreased total sales, and the consumers pay through higher product prices and reduced availability. If the demand for the product is comparatively inelastic, that is, the quantity demanded is comparatively unresponsive to changes in price, then the customers will pay the biggest portion of the tax through higher product prices. Producers will be able to raise their prices without losing a large volume of business. On the other hand, if the demand for the product is fairly price elastic, if the response of quantity demanded is sensitive to price changes, then suppliers will not be able to raise their prices very much without losing a lot of business. The increased cost in this case will cause major reductions in output. Many firms will leave the industry, and those that remain will find their profits greatly reduced or destroyed. Only the very most efficient producers will be able to stay in business. These statements about who pays the tax are equally valid for other kinds of taxes as well. Given a market operation, the impacts of taxes will reverberate throughout the economy and *not* stop with just the guy who gets slapped with the tax itself.

The second category of taxes to be considered is the sales tax. This is known by other names as well, like "excise tax" or "unit tax" or a host of others. Basically, it is a tax on *transactions*, a tax on the process of exchange. Again, it won't make any great difference who actually collects the money and gives it to the government. The seller can or the buyer can. Either way, the one who actually *pays* will again depend upon the elasticities of supply and demand for the product being bought and sold. Often, people think that a sales tax is necessarily *regressive*. While many sales taxes *are* regressive, they don't have to be any more than an income tax has to be progressive. Sales taxes are paid by anyone buying the product as well as the producer of the product. Incidentally, when we talk of the producer of the product bearing a share of the tax, you must realize that the factors hired by the producer will also bear a share of the tax burden. More money being paid in taxes means less money to be shared by the factors of production.

Sales taxes are often levied on basic purchases that make up a large portion of the budgets of low-income families. In this case, a sales tax is regressive in that a larger proportion of low-income budgets is spent on taxable items than is the case for high-income budgets. Therefore, the proportion of income the poorer consumer pays in taxes is greater. This does not have to be the case, however. Consider a sales tax on just luxury goods. We'll put a high sales tax on Rolls Royces while leaving cheap Chevies and VW's tax free. Would this sales tax tend to be regressive? Certainly not! Again, sales taxes can be made to hit whatever group you wish to hit. Like any other tax, however, you must be able to estimate where the actual impact will fall.

Our final category of taxation includes taxes on property holdings. As stated before, this kind of tax is different in that it is a tax on a *stock* of something rather than a *flow* of resources. When one thinks of a property tax, it is generally in the context of a *real estate* property tax. These include taxes on homes, farm land, development land, factory buildings, etc. Generally the tax is levied based on the *value* of the property, and one pays a percentage of that value each year for the privilege of ownership. Again, tracing the actual impact of such taxes is far from simple. Take a tax on homes in a given area, for example. If these taxes go up, the cost of home ownership in the area goes up. This can cause an increase in the demand for homes in adjacent areas where taxes are lower. However, if the increase in taxes means better schools, families may be attracted to the area, particularly families with school-age children. Much of the primary and secondary education in this country is presently financed by property taxes. This means that the cost of education is not necessarily borne by those using the educational facilities. Instead, it is borne by the property owner. Property owners in an area may be a very different population than the parents of school-age children. This has some interesting political effects when an increase in property taxes is put before the electorate. Those receiving the immediate benefits from the taxes are not the ones that are voting to pay or not pay the tax. Many a school district has been deprived from needed funding because of this simple fact of life. As we get farther into the 1970's, the property tax is becoming increasingly unpopular as a method of financing education. Alternative means must be found, but this won't reduce the financial burden of education. It will merely shift the load from one back to another.

What about government expenditures? We have already talked a little about government *fiscal policy*. Fiscal policy concerns what the government, particularly the federal government, does about *taxes* and *government spending*. Increasing taxes tends to decrease the purchasing power of those taxed. This, in turn, will reduce the demand for normal or superior goods demanded by that group of taxpayers. In other words, the government can reduce total (aggregate) demand in the economy by increasing taxes on the demanders. If there is particular pressure on demand in the machine tool and capital goods sector of the economy, an increased tax on business enterprises using these goods might ease the pressure. If there is "excess demand" in the consumer goods sector, an increase in individual income taxes might do the job. If nothing is done, such excess demand will cause inflation in the same way that increasing the money supply in the country would cause inflation. Taxes have been used as a tool to reduce inflationary pressures in times of excess demand.

We have already talked a bit about government expenditures. The importance of knowing whether a government expenditure would represent "new" demand or merely replace private demand was pointed out. Two other aspects of government purchases should be mentioned briefly. First of all, in times of unemployment, the suggestion is often made that the government should have massive programs of hiring people just to do *something*, never mind what, but something. The idea is that even if people just dig holes and fill them up again, this will give an excuse to pay people, the pay they receive becomes buying power, and the buying power stimulates industry to produce. Increased production means increased jobs, and the economy is off and running again. One big problem with this process is that the *product* being produced (refilled holes) isn't really demanded by the economy. If you want to get buying power into the economy, why not produce something that *is* wanted. If the unemployment is the result of unsalable skills or no skills among the unemployed, then the answer is to train or retrain this group of people.

Finally, government expenditures may actually be *investment*. Certainly, many of the education expenditures are really investments in the future productivity of the economy.

Expenditures that truly represent investment have a distinct advantage over expenditures which merely use up resources to provide immediate services. Like any other investment, a government investment will mean an increase in the productivity of the economy at some future time.

Questions and Problems for Chapter 14

1. In the text, the statement was made that both producers and buyers will pay for any tax imposed on the production or sale of a product. The degree to which the tax burden will fall on the buyer will depend partially on how badly he wants the product—how *inelastic* his demand for the product is. See if you can figure out why this is the case.

2. States have used the tax on property as a primary source of funds to finance education—particularly secondary education. Discuss among yourselves who the net beneficiaries of this policy are and who actually pays for it.

3.   List all the functions you think government should perform, particularly those functions which affect the workings of the economy. What effect will these "desirable" functions have on the operation of the market system? How will your ideal government affect your everyday life?

4.   If anyone in your class believes in the necessity of a violent revolution to straighten things out in the world, discuss with him (or her or them) how he would have the post-revolutionary world organized. Who would make the decisions and who would enforce them?

5.   What alternatives can you think of to the use of profits in making production and allocation decisions? List some advantages and disadvantages to these alternatives.

6.   See if you can figure out some of the relative advantages and disadvantages of using so-called fiscal policy or monetary policy in controlling inflation. Get your instructor to lead this one.

7. What are the potential effects on the market economy if political and economic power is concentrated in (a) labor unions, (b) industry groups, (c) the federal government, (d) state and local governments, (e) a handful of rich people, (f) yourself?

8. What do you think would be the effects of a single tax on all purchases—a gigantic sales tax on everything?

9. What would happen if a flat-rate personal income tax was imposed with *no* deductions and *no* exemptions?

10. What is the incentive toward reduced family size provided by our present income tax system?

You'll notice that all of our discussion about the economy as a whole has carefully avoided the issue of what happens when there is trade *outside* the economy. The assumption thus far has been that all economic activity takes place *within* the economic system, nothing comes in from the outside or leaves for the outside—no imports or exports. Now it's time to relax that assumption and see just what are the implications of trading with other countries.

In Figure 15.1, the closed circuit diagram from Chapter 13 is reproduced, but with an important difference. Now we have allowed the flow of materials and services to and from the domestic economy to the rest of the world. You'll notice that there are two arrows going in opposite directions connecting the production sector with the foreign countries. Now goods can be produced in this country to go to consumers, investors (capital goods for use in the production sector itself), inventories, and *exports* to other countries. The rest of the world can provide our economy with imports which can go to the production sector or the consumption sector. By definition, nothing can be "exported" from the consumption sector since it has nothing to sell—it only uses. True, we "export" tourists to other countries where they consume those countries' goods and services. This, however, is just a special kind of "import."

You will notice that the money flows have been omitted from this illustration. This is only to simplify the diagram. As always, money will flow in the opposite direction to goods and service flows. In addition, dollars will flow back into the country to pay for the exports. Right now we can mention one big difference between *domestic trade* and *foreign trade*—the fact that different monies have to be exchanged as well as different goods. Whether you realize it or not,

Figure 15.1
The Economy with Foreign Trade

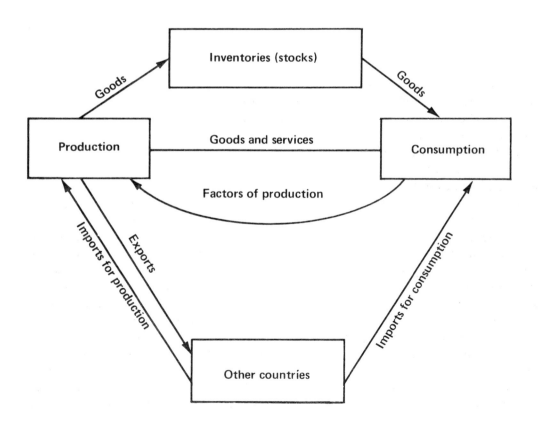

a U.S. dollar will only buy goods and services in the United States. If you go to London, a shopkeeper might accept a dollar bill in exchange for some particular purpose, but the only reason he will is because he knows that it's possible to trade the dollar bill for British currency (pounds sterling). A dollar bill won't generally buy British goods unless it is first converted into British pounds. The same holds true for British pounds purchasing U.S. goods. U.S. goods must be paid for in U.S. dollars. If the British want to buy U.S. goods, they must find someone willing and able not only to sell the *goods*, but also sell them the needed U.S. currency to pay for the goods. The U.S. currency must be paid for by the currency of Great Britain—pounds sterling. What on earth would any seller of dollars want with British pounds? They can't be used to purchase U.S. goods. The answer is simple. If I sell dollars and receive pounds in payment, those pounds are valuable—in fact, required—if I am to buy British goods. The quantity supplied of U.S. dollars will come from U.S. importers of British goods who will use the British pounds to purchase the British goods. The opposite is true for British importers of U.S. goods. They will require U.S. dollars to pay for the goods they import. They will buy the U.S. dollars in return for British pounds. Figure 15.2a illustrates the point. U.S. importers sell U.S. dollars and receive British pounds in payment. The British pounds are then used to pay for the British goods imported into the U.S. At the same time, British importers sell British pounds and receive U.S. dollars in payment. These dollars are then used to pay for the importation of U.S. goods.

What we are implying is that there is a *market* for foreign exchange. This market will reflect the supply of and demand for U.S. dollars and (in the case of Britain) the supply of and demand for British pounds. These supplies and demands in turn reflect the supply of and demand for U.S. and British products being traded. The greater the *demand* for British goods in this country, the greater will be the *supply* of U.S. dollars in the foreign exchange market. The greater the demand for U.S. goods in Britain, the larger will be the supply of British pounds in the exchange market.

If and only if the price of each currency in terms of the other is *pegged*, that is, set artificially, there can be shortages and surpluses of one or the other currency in the world markets. Such artificial prices of currency may make it appear that the prices of goods in each country are different than they actually are. For example, if there is a price of $2.50 for each pound purchased from Great Britain, this means that 2 1/2 U.S. dollars will purchase what one British pound will purchase *in Britain*. What if this dollar price of pounds is artificially high? Suppose the free market price of pounds would be only $1.25 per pound. If the pound is *overpriced* in terms of dollars, this means that British goods will also be *overpriced* in terms of dollars. It's just that simple. But look at this situation from the standpoint of a Britisher interested in buying U.S. goods. If the dollar price of pounds is $2.50, then the pound price of dollars must be the reciprocal of that figure—1/2.5 or .4 pounds per dollar. Again, if the dollar price of pounds in the free market would be $1.25 per pound, then the pound price of dollars

Figure 15.2
Trade and Payment Plans

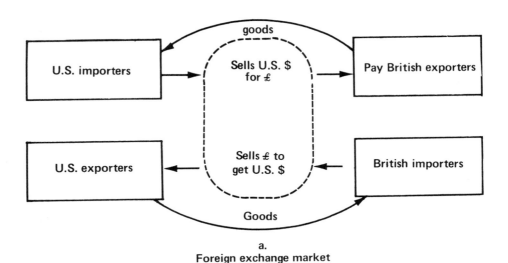

a.
Foreign exchange market

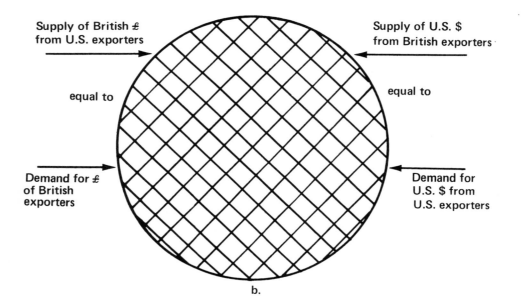

b.

in the free market should be 1/1.25, or .8 pounds per dollar. Obviously, this means that a Britisher is going to look at U.S. goods and consider them a very good bargain indeed. U.S. dollars are *underpriced* in terms of pounds, and therefore U.S. goods are also underpriced in terms of pounds.

I think you can see what will happen. The British will import U.S. goods like crazy. This will raise the quantity of British pounds supplied to the international currency market. At the same time, however, the U.S. demand for the overpriced British goods will be very small, which means that the supply of U.S. dollars to the international currency market will be very small. There will be a *surplus* of pounds and a *shortage* of dollars. Since the dollar price of pounds (and therefore the pound price of dollars) is fixed, this surplus of pounds will just get worse. Britain will suffer from a *balance of payments deficit*. The U.S. will have a *balance of payments surplus*. All this means is that Britain is buying too great a value of U.S. goods *or* that Britain isn't exporting enough goods to the U.S. *or* a combination of the two. Of course, if prices rise in the U.S., the bargain for Britain will become less. If the price rise in the U.S. is not going on in Britain too, then the British goods will start looking better to U.S. customers. Of course, the whole balance of payments problem wouldn't even come up *if* the prices of foreign exchange (the price of one money in terms of the other) were allowed to find their free market equilibrium level. Politics, not economics, makes this simple solution unlikely at this time.

Particularly after looking as some of the financial problems involved with international trade, one might be tempted to ask the simple question, "Why bother with international trade at all? Why not close our borders to all trade and make do with what we make here at home?" The most important answer to this question goes back to the presentation in Chapter 5, when the reasons for specialization and trade were first discussed. Basically the point was made that if one person can make something cheaper (in terms of his own cost) than another person can make it in terms of the other person's cost, it can pay both people to follow their comparative advantages. They should specialize in doing the things that they can each do *comparatively* the best and trade with each other to obtain their non-specialty requirements.

The same reasoning applies to trade between nations. The laws of comparative advantage hold just as true for this kind of trade as they do for trade between individuals. Even if one nation is *absolutely* terrible in terms of their efficiency in the production of *all* goods, specialization in the production of the good that they make relatively the best (or relatively the least worse) will still pay. Perhaps an example will illustrate the point a bit more clearly. Assume that Japan can produce both transistors and automobiles much more efficiently than can the U.S. By this, I mean that the total man-hours and other inputs required to produce both items is *less* in Japan than in the U.S. Should Japan trade with the U.S. (or should the U.S. trade with Japan)? Notice that both questions here are the *same* question. Trade is at least a two party deal. If the U.S. trades with Japan (voluntarily, that is), it must be a good deal for both the U.S. and Japan, or one of the partners would refuse to trade. This point is often overlooked. The existence of trade, at least trade without coercion, is indisputable evidence that each partner at least *believes* that he is benefitting from such trade. Well, back to our question of whether Japan and the U.S. should trade.

The question has nothing to do with the absolute cost of producing either commodity in either country. The question is how much of the alternative product must the U.S. give up to produce one unit of the other product. The same question must be answered in Japan. As long as the cost is *comparatively* different in the two countries, both can gain by specializing and doing that in which it has a comparative advantage.

Let's assume for the moment that it turns out that Japan, although they have absolute advantages in producing both items, has a comparative advantage in the production of transistors. This means automatically that Japan has a *comparative* disadvantage in producing automobiles—comparative to the U.S. This also means that the U.S. has a *comparative* advantage in the production of automobiles and a *comparative* disadvantage in the production of transistors. Remember, the U.S. has an *absolute* disadvantage in the production of both items. If the U.S. takes its resources out of the production of transistors and puts these resources into the production of automobiles, it will then be using its resources as efficiently as possible. For comparable efficiency, Japan would produce just transistors. The two would then trade with each other to obtain the alternative products. By doing this, the *cost* of transistors in terms of the *automobiles foregone* will be less in the U.S. Similarly, the *cost* of automobiles in terms of transistors foregone will be less in Japan. Both countries can benefit by the specialization and trade. They can both be better off than had each produced both items at home. The actual trading price and who will benefit *the most* will depend on other factors, but both will benefit at least a little if they trade at all.

This is fine on paper, but what if you're a worker in a transistor factory in the U.S. or an automobile worker in a factory in Japan. Probably you're going to take a rather dim view of the whole procedure since the kind of specialization envisaged here will put you out of work. This is probably true, but the question is what to do about it.

The most common reaction is to suggest *restricting* the importation of that cheap stuff from abroad. This can be done in several ways, the most common of which is to impose a tax on each unit that comes into the country. Such a tax is called an *import tariff*. It can be imposed as so much *per unit* of the good or so much *per dollar value* of the good. Either way, the imposition of such a tax raises its cost to customers in the U.S. and makes the price of the U.S.-produced good relatively more attractive. The higher price will reduce the sales of the foreign item and increase the sales of the domestic item. Factors of production involved in producing this good will find more demand for their services with the resulting increase in wages and employment. The same sort of thing happens if an *import quota* is established, limiting the quantity of the foreign good that can legally be imported into the country. Again, restricted supply of the import will raise its U.S. price and make the U.S. good relatively more attractive. There are dozens of other gimmicks that governments can use to restrict trade and protect domestic industry. All are after the same thing—to reduce imports and raise the relative cost of buying the import as compared to the domestically produced alternative. Why not do this? If it benefits U.S. citizens, why not? Why should we provide a good market for the cheap foreign products?

Let's see what else has been happening as we restricted the imports of foreign goods. Go back to the example of the U.S. and Japan producing autos and transistors. Assume the transistor industry in the U.S. were able to get the congress to put a limitation on the number of Japanese transistors allowed into the U.S. each year. Such a limitation will raise the price of transistors in the U.S. Yes, this benefits the people producing U.S. transistors, but how about the U.S. citizens that are *buying* transistor products? These people will clearly have to pay a higher price than they would have under free trade. In most cases, the extra resources represented by the increased cost of transistors is *greater* than the extra resources earned by the transistor industry because of the trade restriction. In other words, it would be *possible* to remove all the restrictions from the international (and domestic, too) trade, let the price find its market level, tax all the users of transistors, give this tax to the factors of production in the transistor industry, and still come out better than restricting the trade. The factors could make *more* and the transistor users pay *less* than is the case under the conditions of restricted trade.

Another effect of the trade restriction will also soon be felt. Remember, the only way that Japan can buy our autos is with dollars they get from selling us stuff. If we restrict the import of their transistors, they will have reduced funds with which to buy our cars. The automobile industry, which in this example is our most efficient industry, will lose business, suffer falling profits and prices, and probably have to reduce wages and level of employment of the factors used to make cars. *Protection* of the transistor industry leads inevitably to damaging the industry which is producing for export. Instead of protecting our industries with comparative disadvantages, why not encourage the transfer of these factors into industries which *have* comparative advantages in the world markets? Such a policy can help *all* citizens of the U.S. (and elsewhere, for that matter) more than trade-destroying restrictions and taxes. There is one other probable effect of a U.S. trade restriction on imports. Most likely, Japan will be most unhappy with this action and do a little restricting of her own. Not only will her ability to buy U.S. goods fall because of the fewer dollars available, but Japan will probably *retaliate* for our restrictions by restricting (or further restricting) the inflow of U.S. goods. This can start another round of restrictive measures until trade disappears.

Questions and Problems for Chapter 15

1. List some of the differences and similarities between trade among countries, trade among sectors of a given country, and trade among individuals.

2. Overpriced dollars in terms of German marks means that U.S. goods are overpriced in Germany and German goods are underpriced in the U.S. Explain.

3. A very small percentage of total U.S. economic activity involves foreign trade. Therefore, it is unimportant what happens to our foreign trade program. Comment.

4. I saw a bumper sticker the other day pleading to keep cheap Italian shoes out of the country. The bumper sticker was on the bumper of a Volkswagen. Comment.

5.   Discuss what would happen if all markets in foreign exchange were allowed to operate in a free and uncontrolled fashion. Do you think international trade would increase or decrease? Do you think the world as a whole would be better off or worse off? Why?

6.   Discuss the short- and long-run effects of our giving wheat to India. In this case, assume that we are *giving* it and will not be paid back. What are the effects on (a) the Indian consumer (now and later), (b) the American wheat producer, (c) the Indian wheat producer, (d) the Indian fertilizer manufacturer (e) the U.S. taxpayer.

7.   "The U.S. needs to protect its industries from foreign competition in case we need these industries in time of war." Comment.

8. "The U.S. laborer pays for the importation of cheap foreign-made products." Comment.

9. "We can live by ourselves and to hell with trading with the rest of the world." Comment.

10. "America, love it or leave it." What are the economic implications of this statement?

Postscript

Well there! You've finished. Now you're all economists ready to go out in the world and slay the dragon of scarcity. Of course, you won't succeed. At least, for many people, you won't succeed. The best that can be hoped is that you develop your minds and thinking processes sufficiently to *attack* the dragon in an effective manner. Maybe you can't *kill* him, but you can put an awful dent in him!

Man today has developed the technology of doing things and making things to a degree that was virtually inconceivable 50 to 100 years ago. It has been said that *all* of man's knowledge (I have no idea how to measure "all of man's knowledge") has doubled in the last twenty or thirty years—all knowledge since recorded history began. It is questionable whether man's *wisdom*—his ability to *use* that knowledge—has grown as well.

There is no way that either the book you have just read or the course you have just completed will make you *wise*. What both *can* do if you let them is to open a very small crack in the door to knowledge about one phase of man's existence, his life in a world of scarcity. If you keep working at it, you can pry that door open even wider than others have opened it before. If man is indeed a "special" creature on this earth, one of the "special" characteristics must be his ability to think and reason. This ability can be ignored, used to destroy man, or raise him to accomplishments in all fields that would stagger today's imaginations. It's your choice.